# Principles of Piano Technique and Interpretation

by
Kendall Taylor

**NOVELLO** London and Sevenoaks

£10.95

Cover: Portrait of author by B Jakac

© Novello & Company Limited 1981

1st Reprint (with corrections) 1983

2nd Reprint 1986

3rd Reprint (with corrections) 1993

All Rights Reserved

Printed in Great Britain by Halstan & Co. Ltd.,
Amersham, Bucks.

Cat.No.10 0242

ISBN 0 8536 0073 2

# Contents

# Author's Notes

1    American and European time-values have been used throughout. The equivalents with British names are:

| | |
|---|---|
| whole-note | semibreve |
| half-note | minim |
| quarter-note | crotchet |
| eighth-note | quaver |
| sixteenth-note | semiquaver |
| thirty-second-note | demisemiquaver |
| sixty-fourth-note | hemidemisemiquaver |

2    The right pedal is here always called the sustaining pedal, though often known as the damper pedal.

3    The abbreviations R.H. for right hand and L.H. for left hand have been used throughout.

                                                  K.T.

# Preface

This book is essentially a practical guide, and if it can stimulate and encourage the young performer and those embarking on a teaching career to give systematic and constructive thought to all the processes of learning, from the preliminary stages through to the building-up of an imaginative and mature interpretation, then its purpose will have been achieved. I hope also that it may help the gifted amateur towards greater enjoyment.

A general survey of pianistic problems and of the approach to the vast subject of musical interpretation has been attempted − in terms that will, I trust, not be found too technical. Many of the views expressed are personal, and it is not expected (nor is it desirable) that the intelligent young musician will unquestioningly accept every statement that is made; but it is important that he or she should have an enquiring mind and a satisfactory foundation for personal conclusions on the many points raised.

Some of the topics dealt with in the following pages merit whole volumes to themselves. One such is the difficult subject of the tonal and physiological implications of the pianist's touch. The possibilities of detailed motivic analysis in piano music also remain to be more fully explored; and it was tempting to give more examples (with comments) with regard to the shaping of phrases. I hope however that adequate pointers have been given.

The talented and serious student is expected to be completely dedicated to music (otherwise he should not contemplate making a professional career of it) but it sometimes happens that even a genuinely gifted young musician will tacitly assume that 'playing the piano' is not a notably intellectual pursuit, and that it is enough to develop a brilliant technique and to be generally sensitive and responsive to music. True, sensitivity is a *sine qua non* − and I suggest that an appreciation of other arts such as poetry, painting and architecture will widen the musician's horizon and may well heighten his (or her) awareness of the subtleties of rhythm, colour and structure. Great music however demands something more. Such masterpieces as many of the later works of Beethoven, and Bach's *B minor Mass* and his *St Matthew Passion* offer a direct challenge to one's spiritual values − and in mentioning these works it must be stressed that the pianist should not restrict himself to a knowledge of piano music only. If we accept that the mature work of a great creative genius is a manifestation of one of the highest of all forms of human activity, being a fusion of vision, emotion and intellectual perception, then it follows that to comprehend, and to enrich one's experience of life itself through such an art as music, the mind must be fully engaged as well as the emotions and the senses.

In the preparation of this book my warmest thanks are due to my friends Mrs Eileen Reynolds for many valuable suggestions and to Mr Cameron Taylor for much-appreciated help with the section on piano technique. I am also deeply indebted to Mr Michael Easton of Novello's for the initial suggestion to write such a book and for his encouragement throughout the labour of compiling it; and I would like to thank Mr Desmond Ratcliffe for his expert and patient editing and proof-reading.

Kendall Taylor

To my pupils, past and present

Kendall Taylor

'To teach is to learn'

(Japanese proverb)

*Calligraphy by Tsuneo Kurahashi*

# CHAPTER I

# Preliminary survey: from Bach to Beethoven

Keyboard technique from Bach to Beethoven is a vast subject, ranging as it does throughout the eighteenth century. By the end of that century a true pianistic style had emerged. This, evolved from a technique suitable for the earlier keyboard instruments, now had its own identity. Further developments in keyboard treatment were to come in the next century from the romantic group and from more recent composers. Before reviewing the eighteenth century from the musical angle it may give a certain perspective if we consider briefly the historical background against which the many musical changes were taking place.

If we except the arts and cultures of the East, Europe was the centre of the civilized world, emerging as it was from a largely feudal system. Scientific knowledge was growing; it was not long since Copernicus, Gallileo and Kepler had by their discoveries provided the basis for modern astronomy; a little later Isaac Newton revolutionized scientific thought. The philosophers John Locke, Immanuel Kant and others were questioning established beliefs and established authority.

In the practical field geographical discoveries were still being made, and new wealth was being created from trade with distant parts of the world; arising from this a new class of wealthy and influential merchants and traders was growing. It is noteworthy that in the course of time some members of this new class became patrons of the arts. With a degree of new affluence came the demand for better and more wide-spread opportunities for education, and writers with liberal views were encouraging the masses of the people to think for themselves. Thus it arose that the eighteenth century came to be known as the Age of Reason, and prominent names associated with 'the Enlightenment' include Rousseau (himself a musician), Voltaire and Goethe, the great German poet and philosopher.

These developments were reflected in the arts, and music was much influenced by them. Mention may be made of the *Sturm und Drang* movement which reached its peak in the 1770s; this was a movement holding that the storms and stresses of life should be expressed in the arts, and it was a challenge and a protest against the conventional ornamentation and 'prettiness' of the prevailing rococo style. Among musicians the *Sturm und Drang* movement strongly affected Joseph Haydn; and in its influence on literature and painting it supplied much of the impetus leading to the full flowering of the romantic age at the end of the eighteenth century (and which continued to flourish throughout the nineteenth century). Prominent literary figures of the Romantic Age who worked in or were born in the latter part of the eighteenth century include William Blake (poet and painter), Byron, Shelley and Keats, whilst among the romantic painters were Goya, Turner and Delacroix.

It is significant that in music the towering genius of Beethoven (b. 1770) was to be the bridge leading from the classical purity of Mozart to the romantic freedom of the next century. Unique as he was Beethoven can therefore be regarded as a 'child of his time'. *En passant*, it is salutary to read (with regard to the appeal of music to the masses and the respect given to the passing of a great man) that on the death of Beethoven a crowd of over twenty thousand followed his funeral in Vienna – and that city was then much smaller than now.

Turning to our special subject of keyboard music and keyboard technique from the time of J.S. Bach in the early years of the eighteenth century, we find a strong move towards Equal Temperament in the tuning of keyboard instruments though it may be noted that it was still many years before organs were tuned according to this system. Bach was not the inventor of this method of tuning (there is evidence of experiments with it long before), but he did a great deal towards establishing it. With the previous 'mean-tone' system certain intervals (and certain keys) are in perfect tune, but others are unpleasantly out of tune and therefore virtually unusable. With Equal Temperament a slight artificial adjustment is made; intervals which were formerly in perfect tune lose their purity, but as recompense the whole range of chromatic keys becomes usable. This is a case of compromise where the advantages outweigh the disadvantages. Bach showed his views in a practical manner by writing his two books of Preludes and Fugues in all keys (*Das Wohltemperierte Klavier*).

The general adoption of Equal Temperament opened up the way to the development of the Sonata First Movement principle, an essentially dramatic form with its first and second subject groups in contrasted keys and a development section that is free to modulate. J.S. Bach's most eminent son, C.P.E. Bach, is credited with the development of this principle, which was brought near to perfection by Haydn and Mozart, and later enlarged and used with ever greater freedom by Beethoven.

In the early years of the eighteenth century the keyboard instruments mainly in use were the organ, the harpsichord and the clavichord. The other families of musical instruments, the strings, woodwind and brass were much as they are today (with certain modifications, notably in the brass). These last-mentioned instruments, and the human voice, all share the capacity to make expressive dynamic changes and gradations of tone by varying strengths of bowing or by wind pressure. Of the old keyboard instruments the clavichord alone is capable of subtle tonal gradations, but with its tiny range of sound it is scarcely suitable for public performance even in a small auditorium. The harpsichord, by the nature of its mechanism cannot make tonal differences by touch alone, but by varied registration (stops and couplings) it can make effective contrasts of sound in tonal blocks (widely known as 'terraced dynamics'). Expressive gradations in shaping a melodic phrase are however not possible. In consequence of this limitation the demand arose, in those days when domestic music was becoming available to larger numbers of the population, for a keyboard instrument with a mechanism that would enable the player to vary his tone according to his mood and (more practically) according to the strength of his touch.

It was in response to this call that experiments were made in the early 1700s, and the Italian harpsichord maker Cristofori produced the first workable action that could control tone by the speed with which a hammer (instead of a plectrum, which in the harpsichord is a quill) hits the strings. Cristofori's action was the direct ancestor of the mechanism of the modern piano. The tonal quality of the early pianos was however not appealing and Bach, on hearing one, declined to use it. Nevertheless the new instrument continued to be developed, and Silbermann and Streicher were noteworthy in improving both the tonal quality and the mechanism in the middle years of the eighteenth century; but it was not until the late 1770s that the tone quality was sufficiently good to tempt the composers of the day, notably Haydn and Mozart, to write for the new forte-piano instead of the harpsichord for their keyboard works. It is to be noted that some years afterwards Haydn refused a commission to write a sonata for harpsichord saying that after writing for the forte-piano he could not return to the harpsichord style. It is also interesting that for nearly thirty years afterwards the music publishers of the period insisted upon presenting works as 'For Harpsichord or Forte-piano', realizing that the homes of many music-lovers would still contain only harpsichords; even Beethoven's Sonata, Op. 27, No. 2 (known as *The Moonlight* and published in 1802) comes into this category, though it was certainly not intended for the harpsichord.

Mozart, born in 1756, was brought up as a harpsichordist and though the later keyboard works of his short life were written for forte-piano, we read that whilst his playing was greatly admired for its taste and clarity it was not remarkable for its legato quality. It would seem that he continued to use the technique of the harpsichord when playing the forte-piano. It will be realized that the quill of a harpsichord produces clear articulation in passage-work of rapid notes but, though legato can be produced on the harpsichord, the plucking of the strings by the quill does not produce the same smooth effect as the mechanism of hammers and dampers in legato-playing on the piano. This difference when applied to the performance of harpsichord music on the piano suggests that, as a matter of style, we should not aim to produce the same kind of legato as when playing the works of composers of the romantic period such as Chopin who wrote with the special qualities of the piano in mind.

With the advent of Beethoven a true piano style and technique were established. Beethoven's playing is said to have been dynamic and dramatic, with free use of arm-movement in producing tone. In his keyboard works we find, even in the earliest sonatas, virtuoso passages (as in the C major Sonata of Op. 2, dating from 1794−5) setting new standards of technical brilliance and difficulty. It must not however be forgotten that Haydn (b. 1732) in his last sonatas for piano, written in England in 1794, also realized fully the tonal possiblities of the piano and, as an example, his magnificent Sonata in E flat, Hob. 52 calls for great breadth of style and as wide a range of tone as anything in the first period of Beethoven's keyboard works.

The foundations of modern piano technique may therefore be said to have been laid down by the end of the eighteenth century and in the early years of the nineteenth century. Such works as Beethoven's *Hammerklavier* Sonata, Op. 106 still tax the technical equipment as well as the intellectual and emotional grasp of the virtuosi of today. Nevertheless, Chopin and Liszt (in their Studies and other works), and Brahms (notably in his Paganini Variations) invented new technical devices, whilst Debussy found new sonorities to add to the repertoire of pianistic colours and effects.

CHAPTER II

# Principles of piano technique

Before tabulating the physical movements called for in a comprehensive technique it may be helpful to outline the possibilities of tone-production and tonal variety by normal use of keyboard and pedals; coupled with this one must be aware of the basic facts connected with a pianist's touch.

The piano is essentially a percussive instrument in that tone is produced by the hammers striking the strings. The speed of the hammer blow directly determines the amount of tone produced (note that in this case speed is synonymous with strength or force). The hammer has a fixed trajectory, and the working of the action of the piano 'throws' the hammer against the string, from which it rebounds instantly. In consequence of this action the only variable factor possessed by the hammer is that of speed, hence a slow-moving hammer produces soft tone and a fast-moving hammer loud tone (with all the infinite variety of speeds, and therefore of degrees of tone, in between).

The quality (as distinct from quantity) of tone can, in the case of a single note, only be varied to the extent that it may be spoilt by the added extraneous noise of too percussive an attack. It would appear that it is only in the relationship of sounds heard either consecutively as in a sensitively graded melody, or together as in well-balanced harmony, that tone can begin to have a 'personal' quality.

From the above it will be realized that the piano can also be regarded as percussive because in certain types of touch the player's fingers 'strike' the keys. To strike the key from a distance, without preparation on the key-surface, sets the key and the action into motion with a sudden jerk causing not only the percussive thud of the finger-tip making contact but adding also percussive and frictional noises from the mechanism; these undesirable sounds are heard at their maximum if the player approaches the key with a rigid wrist (a flexible wrist can act as a shock-absorber enabling the percussive element to be modified). The listener's ear registers the result of an over-percussive touch as 'hard' or harsh tone.

The percussive style of writing for the piano has been much exploited by some twentieth-century composers but it will be realized that percussive effects (generally in connection with some form of staccato) are by no means absent in classical and romantic piano writing. The percussive element can be brilliantly effective but its use calls for taste and discretion, comparable to the judicious (and sparing) use of the percussion department by a composer scoring for orchestra. The pianist will find that for most of his playing it is desirable for musical and tonal reasons to try to eliminate or at least to mask this secondary percussive characteristic of the piano, and to create the illusion that the piano can 'sing' a legato melody persuasively; he must also be able to produce a rich sonorous tone in chord passages without 'hardness'. Debussy in *La Cathédrale Engloutie* demands that a fortissimo chord-passage should be 'sonore sans dureté' – and it was said of his own playing that 'he could make one forget that the piano has hammers'.

Turning to a consideration of finger technique, it soon became clear in the latter years of the eighteenth century when the piano gained ascendancy over the harpsichord that the finger action suitable for the light touch of the earlier instrument was not adequate for the heavier mechanism and for the range of tone available on the piano. J. S. Bach is said by Forkel, his first biographer, to have played with an absolutely still hand (except for the lateral movement necessary to cover the compass of the keyboard). Bach used the thumb freely which was not common practice in his time; he also used finger-substitution (changing one finger for another on the same note) in order to join finger-groups, and he often passed a longer finger over a shorter one. The following example is from an *Applicatio in C dur* written as an exercise for his son W. Friedemann Bach; it shows the kind of fingering he expected the boy to learn.

Forkel stated that Bach's finger-action was a flexing or bending of the joints of the fingers in drawing back the tips towards the palm of the hand. Finger touch on the piano requires the more powerful movement of the finger activated as a whole from the knuckle. Tonal range will nevertheless be limited if the player is restricted to finger touch, and to produce a bigger tone he must call on some additional source of energy; this will be energy from the arm.

In preparing to produce a musical sound one must always imagine what amount and what kind of tone will be suitable for the notes or for the passage which is to be played; the need for concentrated and imaginative listening is evident. The intensity of sound required will therefore directly determine the speed to be imparted to the key which in turn controls through the mechanism the velocity with which the hammer hits the strings. In consequence of this necessity to 'control' the speed of the key there must also be a full control of the arm behind the fingers. This control at once rules out the possibility of a completely relaxed fall of the arm; the fully-relaxed 'free' fall of the arm plays no part in piano tone-production. Muscular relaxation is indeed valuable and necessary, but it can only be partial and momentary. The utmost freedom and suppleness of movement of fingers, wrist and arm should not be confused with muscular relaxation. Chopin's constant reminder to his pupils is said to have been: 'Toujours la souplesse'. (See page 13 for comments on the use of the arm.)

In matters relating to the use of fingers, hand, wrist and arm it is important to consider and to apply the laws of mechanics and leverage. The contribution of gravity can be assumed; and in this connection it may be well to recall the usual definitions of elementary physics, i.e. that 'mass' is the amount of material in an object, and that 'weight' is the pull of gravity on that 'mass'.

The weight alone of a finger will not depress a piano key; the weight of the hand and arm, released when the fingers are in contact with the keys and with the wrist well-raised, will only produce un-controlled sound without tonal range; and if the hand and arm are lifted above the keys for an unprepared attack we shall find, as noted above, that on dropping like a falling stone an unpleasantly percussive sound is heard when contact with the key is made − moreover, tone here also is uncontrolled.

It is clear that piano touch involves muscular effort and control. Whatever the touch to be used, the resistance of the piano key causes a reaction or recoil. If a finger touch is used, the downward action of the finger will cause an involuntary lift of the knuckles, wrist and fore-arm; the finger will react, like any other lever, against the base to which it is attached. This reaction may be restrained by conscious muscular effort but it is found that even the most gentle striking of the key, or the slightest pressure applied to it when the finger is already in contact causes, as reaction, signs of upward movement of knuckle, hand, wrist and fore-arm.

From this it follows that to overcome the initial key-resistance a minimal degree of muscular fixation or contraction – of which the player may not be conscious – is needed, but this must be of as short a duration as possible. If the movements associated with touch are accurately timed and well co-ordinated to overcome key-resistance at precisely the right moment then the fixation is so brief that it seemed to early observers that relaxation was unbroken when meeting the key. As we have seen, controlled muscular effort assists gravity; and a brief moment of muscular tension occurs in order to control the reaction caused in overcoming the resistance of the key.

In practical terms, the player should, as stated above, imagine aurally the tone he wishes to produce, and through his experience of piano touch he estimates the speed which he must impart to the key to produce that tone; on his accuracy and judgment in making this estimate depends his success in producing the desired effect.

It is important to realize that 'sound-point' (i.e. that point in the depressing of a piano key when sound is actually heard) is a variable factor depending on key-speed: (a) fortissimo tone is produced by rapid movements of keys, mechanism and hammers; this causes sound to be produced before the key has travelled far below surface-level. It follows that touch for fortissimo may be aimed at a point very little below the key-surface. This has an important influence on passages such as brilliant octaves which need to be loud; because it is not necessary to take time playing deeply into the keys greater velocity can be achieved. A slogan for this approach could well be: 'Solid at the top (of the key) – nothing at the bottom'. Incidentally, a strong blow aimed too deeply into the key will result in the fault known as 'key-bedding' – hammering into the pads below the keys. (b) Conversely, pianissimo tone can be controlled by a slow depressing of the key, transmitted equally slowly through the piano action to the hammer which is given just enough momentum to reach the strings; in this case the key will have travelled further (deeper) before sound is heard. Satisfactory soft tone will not normally be produced therefore with shallow key-depressing, the inference being that the hand and wrist may be held at slightly lower level for quiet playing as compared with forte-playing. A certain complication arises however in connection with the playing of pianissimo passages that require the utmost rapidity (examples are found in Liszt's concert study, *La Leggierezza*). The fingers, playing rapidly in succession, do not in these cases go deeply into the keys for the required pianissimo; in quick progressions from note to note just sufficient impetus must be given to the hammers to ensure that they will reach and strike the strings without force. Remember that the hammers are thrown (or catapulted) against the strings and are not under the player's direct control at the moment of impact. Technical control of a high standard is required to ensure that hammer-speed is evenly matched from note to note; it is only too common to find some notes failing to speak in rapid pianissimo passages whilst others are too loud.

The following table lists the physical movements which a pianist is required to make in acquiring a comprehensive technique. The explanations of these movements have been simplified as much as seems possible consistent with adherence to the principles of tone-production already given.

| | | |
|---|---|---|
| 1 | *Finger-action* | – never forgetting that whatever the touch employed it is the fingers that make contact. |
| 2 | *Use of the arm* | |
| 3 | *Freedom of wrist* | – fingers remaining in contact with the keys whilst the wrist rises and falls in acting as a bridge or hinge between arm and fingers. |

| 4 | *Hand movement* | – as in hand-staccato (frequently called wrist-staccato). An independent movement of the hand from the wrist, generally combined with undulation of the fore-arm. |
| 5 | *Fore-arm martellato action* | |
| 6 | *Rotary movement* | – (Fore-arm rotation) |
| 7 | *Lateral freedom* | |

There must be no gaps in the player's equipment. All the above movements are required in the complete technique; they should in the first place be learnt separately, though in performance they will generally be combined, often in complex fashion. Exercises exploiting them should be part of the student's daily practice both at the keyboard and away from it. (Some examples are given in Chapter III.)

## Posture

Couperin, in his classic work: *The Art of Playing the Harpsichord* (published in 1716), states that for the most efficient use of the fingers one should sit at such a height that the underside of the fore-arm should be parallel to the ground. This implies that with the fingers resting on the already-depressed keys there should be a continuous line to the point of the elbow. This accords well with modern views on height, in posture at the piano; the stool or chair should be adjusted accordingly, both for height and for distance away from the keyboard.

The distance from the keyboard will be such that, sat upright (or leaning only slightly forward from the seat) the upper arms will fall freely from the shoulder with the elbows a little forward from the body. It is assumed that the tips of the longer fingers will just reach to the base of the black keys. (For comments on hand and finger position see below.) If sat too far away the arms will be outstretched, with consequent strain at the shoulders and considerable risk of pain in the back after long hours of practice; in addition, if playing with a relatively straight arm reaching forward from the shoulder, there cannot be a free and independent vertical movement of the fore-arm from the elbow (whilst keeping the fingers on or close to the keys). If, on the other hand, one sits too close to the keyboard, the position will be cramped; with the upper arm hanging vertically from the shoulder it will be impossible to use upper arm leverage (for weighty chords or passages) without lifting or heaving-up the shoulder in ungainly and inefficient fashion.

## Finger-action

In finger-touch the position which is most effective and most economical of energy and effort will be to have an arched hand with knuckles slightly higher than the wrist, whilst the tips of the fingers rest on the key-surface with the nail phalanges of the longer fingers approximately vertical. This position of the fore-arm and hand is easily checked by resting the fore-arm from elbow to wrist on a flat horizontal surface such as a table-top; hold the fingers well-rounded as described above, and note that the back of the hand rises slightly from wrist to knuckles. Experiment has shown that if using a straight finger (moving radially from the knuckle) the energy transmitted to the key is only approximately three-fifths of that produced by the finger playing vertically downward with the finger-tip making contact (this of course implies equal effort used in both cases). The straight finger, moving in a curve from the knuckle, executes a glancing or stroking blow which is relatively inefficient and which also loses a little in friction over the key-surface. The rounded finger which is recommended should maintain this position after playing; it is occasionally noticed that the student immediately straightens his finger after releasing a note; this can cause loss of control and is time-consuming in making unnecessary movement. When possible the fingers should be prepared in groups in advance as in scale-playing (see Chapter IV for further comment on scales and group-fingering). It should incidentally be noted that the finger position recommended applies to 'brilliant' finger-touch and not necessarily to the position or condition of the finger when using the arm in conjunction with the fingers, as often in 'cantabile' and in chord-playing.

If successions of quick notes are to be both fluent and controlled, a balanced or 'floating' arm is required, and just sufficient resistance or fixation is needed from it to provide an adequate base against which the fingers can exert themselves effectively in producing tones of varied intensities in rapid passage-work. The wrist and the elbow are the principal joints concerned, and the distribution of tension between them becomes an important matter for adjustment according to the strength of tone required. Summing up this aspect: in rapid finger-work there will be a balanced arm with the weight kept off the fingers, and the fingers will react against firm knuckles, wrist or elbow according to the degree of exertion.

Frequently it will be found that fatigue can be avoided in continuous rapid finger-work by varying the base against which the fingers react; this, in effect, means employing a different hand, wrist or fore-arm movement behind the fingers according to the changing patterns of the notes. An excellent example of such varied patterns is to be found in Chopin's Etude in C sharp minor, Op. 10, No. 4 where, after a first bar of finger-action almost unaided by other movement, the second bar calls for rotary freedom and the third bar for assistance from free lateral movement.

Ex 2

Weber's *Moto perpetuo* Rondo provides similar changes of technical approach: the fingers will receive rotary assistance in the first pattern; the chromatic scale which follows calls for unaided finger-work, and in the third pattern (from G with sforzando) the fingers will be assisted by undulating fore-arm and wrist movements which help to mark the minor accents at the start of the four-note groups. Without a varied approach the piece would prove unduly tiring.

Ex 3

In the smooth legato that is so frequently required in piano-playing the fingers will remain either fully in contact with the key-surface or will lift only very slightly above it. To produce more tone the fingers, whilst maintaining the well-rounded position, will lift above the keys only as much as may be necessary to generate more speed; the high lift-back of fingers that is sometimes advocated produces tension of hand and wrist. The aim should be to attain ample power and control from as close to the key-surface as possible, thus largely eliminating unnecessary percussive sounds caused by striking from a high finger and, for rapidity in playing, reducing time-consuming movements. It is, incidentally, said that a favourite exercise of Liszt's in cultivating finger-action was to practise slow trills between each pair of fingers, varying and grading the tone but always playing from the key-surface. He insisted on the pupil listening intently to secure a perfect legato with no overlap of sounds nor any gap between them; on releasing each note slowly care had to be taken to ensure that the finger remained in contact with the key as it was allowed to rise. Observers stated of Liszt's own playing in rapid passage-work that it was as if his fingers were glued to the keys.

As the player develops the facility and speed of his finger-work, the principle of the undulating fore-arm and wrist movements should be introduced. This consists of the wrist falling (plus a small measure of downward thrust) to assist the appropriate accentuation of the first note of a rhythmic group, proceeding then to rise gradually until the fingers have played the last note of the group, after which the process is repeated with the wrist (and fore-arm) again falling to assist in the playing of the first note of the next group. Five-finger exercises played with varied accents provide a convenient means of acquiring this skill.

Exercises based on the examples should be played in all keys, and by the L.H. in reverse.

As something of a contrast to the legato described above there are many occasions when separate articulation of finger-work is required. The effect at which to aim will be something closely akin to the separate bowing of string players or the separate tonguing of wind instruments. Most of the running sixteenth-note passages in Mozart's piano concertos and sonatas are not slurred, and they should have a pearl-like clarity of articulation. It is also frequently necessary to give firm separate articulation to sixteenth-note passages in many works of Beethoven, and this type of touch is often needed when playing Bach's keyboard works on the piano.

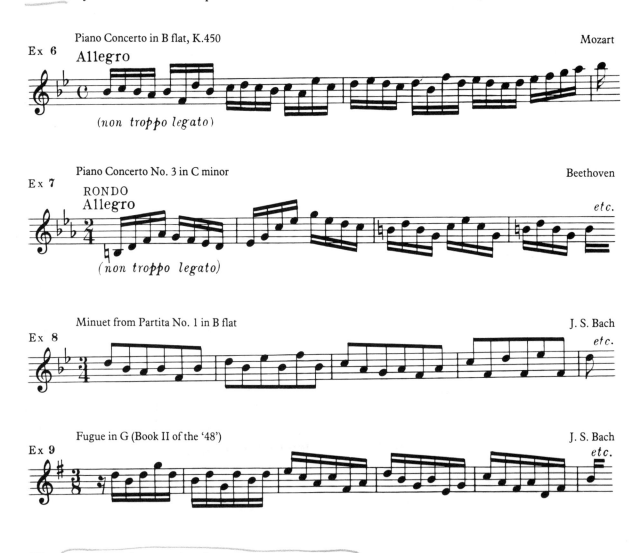

The appropriate finger-action for this 'non troppo legato' articulation must be cultivated; the slow trill exercise recommended by Liszt should now be practised with a deliberate short break between each note:

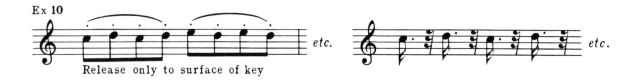

Five-finger exercises, beginning with the simplest of patterns and at first played slowly with detached notes, as for the slow trill exercise, will also help in acquiring a good non legato articulation. Scales also should be practised with non legato touch in addition to the normal legato.

It remains to mention the true finger-staccato touch as distinct from the above non legato. The action of the finger here is best learnt starting with the playing of rapid repeated notes, changing fingers for each repetition. The finger-movement is in this case a 'stroking' of the keys, and finger-staccato is the only type of touch in piano-playing in which such a stroking action is justified. As each note is played the finger concerned is flexed, pulling back towards the palm of the hand so that it strikes a glancing blow in playing and releasing the key with one and the same action. In this there is a saving of time as compared with the normal movements in two directions ('down-up') for each note sounded; a more rapid rate of repetition is therefore available. The finger-action described is similar to that attributed to J. S. Bach as his normal finger-touch.

The pupil should first learn this particular technique using the fingers 4, 3, 2; and for these rapid repeated notes the fingers will strike more on the front edge of keys than is usual (this also applies to the black keys).

When control and facility have been achieved with the three fingers mentioned, the thumb may be added in order to join the groups; this will call for a smooth movement forward into the key in maintaining an even rhythmical pattern of the four repeated notes, and care must be taken to ensure that the thumb in moving forward does not disturb the even and rhythmic action of the other fingers.

The change of finger will be from the fourth and fifth fingers inward towards the index-finger and thumb, except when a single repetition is approached from above; the finger-change can then be from thumb to index-finger. In this case the thumb will fall from the front edge of the key in making way for the following index-finger:

12

Finger-staccato scale and passage-work will also use the same kind of finger-action as that described above; this touch will however be used only for light, rapid passages of staccato in single-notes. Staccato passages requiring more tone, but at a steadier pace, will find hand-staccato or fore-arm-staccato necessary in dealing with other degrees of speed and tone. The light, rapid staccato finger-touch should be learnt using first the three fingers 4, 3, 2. This is precisely as for repeated notes (see above) but now used for three adjacent descending notes (reverse for L.H.):

Ex 14

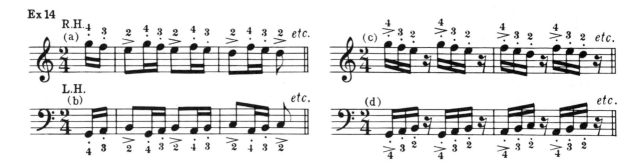

Later, the fifth (little) finger should be added to make the pattern:

Ex 15

As with repeated notes the action of the fingers is restricted to the flexing of the joints in pulling back the tips of the fingers towards the palm of the hand. When the thumb is introduced care must be taken to ensure that the tone and the degree of staccato match and blend perfectly with that produced by the other fingers; an effective vertical movement of the thumb must also be cultivated − the function of the thumb in piano-playing is normally to pass under the hand when connecting finger-groups, or to stretch outward.

Ex 16

Reverting to the changing of fingers when repeating notes, it cannot be emphasized too strongly that this is only necessary in the case of rapid repetitions. For repeated notes of longer value this changing of fingers is entirely unnecessary. The use of the same finger, when repeating at a slower tempo, implies that there will be no change in the angle at which the hand is held relative to the key; control of tone is therefore easier. In these slower examples, such as repeated quarter-notes of a melody, finger-touch *per se* will not be used; the finger will be aided by use of the arm. Many otherwise good editions are badly at fault in marking entirely unnecessary changes of finger for repeated single notes in relatively slow-moving passages; there are also many examples of editorial finger-changes applied to double-notes which make simple repetitions very awkward indeed:

Valse in E flat, Op. 18   Chopin

The changes of finger here are quite wrong and pointless.

## Use of the arm

When considering the development of piano technique from that which was suitable for the harpsichord, the use now made of the arm strikes one as the most important difference. It has however proved difficult to analyse and to define precisely how the arm is used. We find different and sometimes opposed and confusing views expressed in the writings of Matthay, Breithaupt and others on the subject of weight-touch. The difficulty has been to establish the roles played by (a) the 'mass' of the arm falling by gravitation (with the implication of weight released by muscular relaxation); (b) the degree of relaxation that may be possible, considering that tone of a particular intensity must be produced at a precise moment in time (both these requirements of tone and timing stipulate nervous and muscular control that would appear to be the antithesis of 'free fall' relaxation); and (c) the part played by conscious downward thrust of the arm (fore-arm, upper-arm or both in combination) in assisting gravitational fall. It must be remembered also that in overcoming key-resistance there is a measure of recoil (which is quite considerable in the production of forte tone), and this induces a momentary muscular firmness or fixation.

An approach to this problem can be made by asking what it is that we demand of piano tone that unaided finger-action cannot satisfy. A consideration of 'cantabile' (meaning 'songlike') can provide a clue to such a question; as the singing voice is not percussive, the pianist in playing a cantabile melody must use his art and his technique to disguise, as well as he may be able, the percussive aspect of tone-production. Imagine a melody needing a warm and full tone rising, possibly, to a considerable climax: finger-touch alone cannot provide the tonal range nor the right quality of sound; when pressed for more tone, finger-touch becomes markedly percussive (as 'drumming' firmly with the fingers on a table-top will at once establish). Some other source of energy is clearly needed. Secondly, consider also the many heavy chord passages in piano music: such as the opening of Tchaikovsky's First Piano Concerto or, in stylistic contrast, the passage already quoted from Debussy's *La Cathédrale Engloutie* where the composer specifically asks that tone shall not be 'hard' in quality.

It is for such passages that the use of the arm behind the fingers is called upon. As stated earlier, if the fingers strike with force from above the keys there will be, in addition to the thud of the fingers making contact with the key-surface, some extraneous noise from the sudden activation of the mechanism. If however the player commences tone-production with his fingers already in contact with the keys, the percussion of the fingers striking the keys is eliminated, and the piano-action in accelerating from a rest-point produces less mechanical noise.

The act of touch when using the arm actively behind the fingers is a complex one involving a combination of arm, wrist and fingers. The whole arm, reacting against the shoulder, will be involved, but for tone of a moderate intensity the leverage of the fore-arm and the supple rise and fall of the wrist will be the most prominent visible features. For heavier tone there will be, in preparation for tone-production, a more appreciable lifting of the upper arm; the shoulder will not be lifted but there will be some momentary tension there. As the arm lifts so will the wrist rise with complete freedom and suppleness; the longer fingers will remain in contact with the keys, with finger-tips just touching, even

14

when the wrist is at maximum height. Neither the arm nor the wrist remain lifted (which would keep both in a state of tension) but similarly as a conductor's 'up-beat' at once falls to give the inevitably following 'down-beat', so does the shoulder release the arm. The fall of the arm is not however a complete relaxation of effort; for forte tone there will be a precisely-timed downwards thrust assisting the assumed gravitational fall. The arm transfers its energy and weight to the firmly-shaped fingers through the medium of the wrist, which is now pulled downwards by the arm. As the wrist is the bridge or link between the arm and the hand (remembering that the fingers are in contact with the key-surfaces throughout) the wrist itself must be firm at the moment of tone-production to overcome key-resistance, otherwise control of tone will be lacking. A strong enough base must be found to withstand and absorb the strong reaction or recoil arising from the energy expended in forte-playing, and there will be momentary firmness (or fixation) of finger-joints, knuckles and elbow. On completion of tone-production there may be a partial condition of relaxation in the upper arm; when this possibility exists it can only be of the briefest duration as preparation for the next chord or progression will be immediate. For maximum effectiveness there must be an awareness (when using an arm-touch) of the function of the fingers in gripping the keys firmly.

With regard to the desirability, or otherwise, of preparing notes and chords in advance on the key-surface: not only is percussion reduced, but advance preparation makes for greater accuracy and for better control in judging tonal intensity. Only when a percussive effect is called for by the style of writing will there be a justification for lifting the hand and fingers above the keys (see under 'Hand-staccato', p.16 and 'Fore-arm martellato action', p.19).

For 'cantabile' one uses fundamentally the same touch-form as that described above for forte-playing, but modified as to the amount of energy to be expended. There will be complete freedom of wrist and fore-arm in the up-lift before tone-production; the release and controlled down-thrust will be carefully judged and timed according to the amount of tone required – which must always be imagined aurally in advance. With the wrist momentarily raised at the peak of the preliminary up-lift the tip of the finger concerned will be lightly in contact with the key, but as the hand and wrist make their controlled fall the fleshy 'pad' will come in contact as the key is depressed and the sound produced. Tone is governed by the speed at which the fore-arm, wrist and hand are permitted to fall.

The young player in 'singing' a melody with the assistance of the arm must beware of one or two pitfalls: (a) he will, rightly, be aware that once a note on the piano has been sounded, only sufficient pressure is needed just to hold the note down lightly for the necessary time-value; realizing that extra pressure has no influence whatever, he may be tempted to lift the wrist immediately the note has been sounded. With a long-value note it is better to hold the key down lightly at a lower level; the preliminary up-lift and the release to play the following note can then be made in one combined movement at a uniform speed – the speeds of the up-beat and the following down-beat are inseparably linked in conducting, and it is better that they should also be related in playing. (b) One occasionally finds an inexperienced young player mixing his movements from note to note in the playing of a cantabile melody, e.g. producing one tone with the hand and finger falling adequately into the key, only to play the next note in something akin to a 'see-saw' movement with the wrist rising as the finger is pushed forward into the key; naturally enough the two successive tones do not match.

There is a very real difficulty to be understood and overcome in the case of those melodies which include a mixture of long and short value notes, such as quarter-notes and sixteenth-notes. One of many such cases is found in the opening of Chopin's F minor Nocturne. Op. 55:

Ex 18   Andante

In this example the quarter-notes will each have separate hand and fore-arm movements as described above, but the sixteenth-notes will be played with a finger-touch, and very great care must be taken in blending the tone of these quicker notes. The *Largo* slow movement of Chopin's B minor Sonata, Op. 58 contains another difficult example of this same problem:

To blend the notes of this melody of varied time-values, and to give sensitive gradation successfully requires judgment and artistry of a high order.

One further point remains to be mentioned in the case of 'cantabile legato': an artist who knows well what he is doing may deliberately choose to play a legatissimo that includes a minimal overlap of tone. This fractional overlap is designed to cover (or to mask) the hammer-hit of the new note, and the first of the two notes concerned will be damped as soon as possible after the second note is heard. In a normal legato the first note is damped precisely as the second note sounds. Acute listening and split-second timing are vital if this overlap legatissimo is to justify itself; if the damping of the second note is delayed the listener's ear senses an unpleasant blur. A similar legatissimo overlap is sometimes justifiable with the use of the sustaining pedal in chord passages; for examples see the section on pedalling (p.24).

In reviewing the types of passage when the use of arm movement can assist the fingers, mention may again be made of rhythmic accentuation that may be required in running passage-work; an energy-assisted fall of the fore-arm, transferred to hand and fingers through the bridge of the wrist can help the finger to produce any accent that may be required (see Ex. 5 under 'Finger-action'). One of countless such examples is found in Mozart's A major Concerto, K. 488, first movement, bars 86 – 90:

Here the hand rises a little whilst playing the two or three notes preceding the one to be slightly stressed; the assisted fall into the high treble D on the third beat is carefully timed, and the recoil from the extra pressure is borne by the wrist. This is an example of the undulating fore-arm and wrist technique already discussed, and which will be mentioned again when dealing with hand-staccato.

At this stage it must be mentioned that it is possible also to produce tone by thrusting the arm forward into the keys with the wrist (starting from a rather low level) lifting as the arm pushes forward, whilst simultaneously the fingers, which will have been held over the appropriate keys in a flat or straight position, flex and grip the keys firmly. This type of action leaves the hand, wrist and arm in a state of tension *after* tone-production, and it is conducive to key-bedding; it cannot be generally recommended but is occasionally appropriate in dealing with 'sforzandi' on weak beats followed immediately by normal tone-production. Examples are found in Beethoven's *Appassionata* Sonata, Op. 57, in the third movement, bars 98–111, and elsewhere:

Ex 21

Here the sforzando eighth-note chord is played as described above; with the wrist starting from a low level the arm pushes forward vigorously and the wrist in rising impels the fingers down into the keys. The hand falls normally into the next eighth-note chord on the first beat of the next bar.

With the exception of the above relatively rare instance one can conclude that gravitation will always play a part in tone-production assisted by the use of the arm; the gravitational and partially relaxed fall must be controlled according to the intensity of the tone that is required, and a degree of force or thrust will also be needed. The combination of gravity and force is fundamental to the use of the arm. A reminder may not come amiss that as a lever must react against the base to which it is attached, the use of the arm in helping the fingers to overcome key-resistance and to impart speed to the action and hammers will produce a muscular reaction or recoil and thereby call for a momentary firmness or fixation. The student who wishes to probe more deeply into the anatomical and physiological processes involved is recommended to read *The Physiological Mechanics of Piano Technique* by Otto Ortmann (Dutton) to whom we are indebted for his exhaustive experiments and his conclusions in determining various aspects of the relationship between the pianist and his piano.

## Hand-staccato

Hand-staccato is the most frequently used form of staccato touch, offering as it does a considerable range of tone plus the possibility of attaining a very useful degree of velocity. Very rapid and light passages of single notes will be played with a finger-staccato touch; and a fore-arm martellato will provide the power for the brilliant forte octaves (and comparable passages) found in many virtuoso concertos. Hand-staccato (which is sometimes called 'wrist-staccato') will be appropriate for the many passages falling between these extremes. It should be understood at once that whilst it will first be necessary to cultivate an independent movement of the hand from the wrist, any extended passage requiring such a staccato will invariably combine an undulating rise and fall of the fore-arm into which the hand movements 'fit' as a group; without this undulating movement continuous hand-staccato quickly produces tension and rigidity.

The first requisite for learning this type of staccato is to cultivate a free and supple movement of the hand from the wrist. The independence of the movement may easily be checked by placing the fore-arm in contact with a level table or desk surface from elbow to wrist; in this position, move the hand up and down without letting the wrist or fore-arm lose contact with the surface on which the arm is resting. Practise this movement away from the keyboard as if single notes, double notes and chords were being played staccato. Transfer this action to the keyboard and play repeated sixths in C major with thumb and little finger. The wrist and fore-arm will be held on the same level as the keys (as if an extension of them) and the hand will therefore lift slightly higher than the wrist prior to striking the keys.

Ex 22

When facility has been achieved at the keyboard with this independent hand movement, it must be incorporated into the undulating fore-arm principle. Applying this principle: make an exercise of repeated sixths, as above, but now in well-marked rhythmic groups of fours:

The hand and wrist will fall, in playing the first sixteenth-note, to a slightly lower level than is normal; the second, third and fourth sixteenth-notes are to be played with a small amount of independent movement of the hand as the wrist gradually rises before falling again into the first note of the next beat. It is at first advisable to permit a rest-point on the second beat, but as ease and fluency are acquired the 'chain' of notes can be extended to two or three beats of sixteenth-notes. The rhythmic grouping should also be varied to include six notes to the beat:

A common fault in the learning of this compound movement is to let the hand rise too soon; there should be very little lifting of the wrist before the second halves of the groups (whether these be fours or sixes). It should not be necessary to add that intervals other than that of the sixth may also be practised, but a small hand may find difficulty in acquiring freedom and ease with the relatively large interval of an octave.

In rapid repeated-note passages of double notes (such as the notorious octaves in Schubert's *Erlkönig* song accompaniment, Liszt's sixth Hungarian Rhapsody, Schumann's Toccata, etc.) a mastery of the undulating fore-arm principle is necessary in averting or delaying fatigue. Many pianists also prefer to use this particular technique for the playing of repeated single notes, as in the following passage from Beethoven's *Appassionata* Sonata:

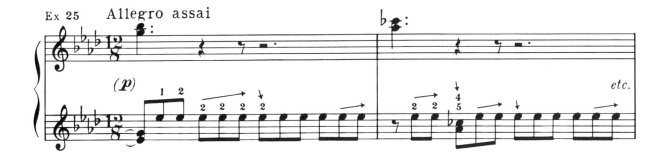

this is eminently practicable at the tempo of this movement, but beyond a certain velocity it becomes necessary to adopt a pattern of changing fingers such as 3 2 1 or 4 3 2 1 for very quick repetitions:

Tarantella (Venezia e Napoli)                                                    Liszt

The undulating principle is not by any means confined to repeated notes, and it will also be applied to such passages as the eighth-note chords of the sixth, in rising scale form, at the opening of the fourth movement of Beethoven's Sonata in C major, Op. 2, No. 3,

and to the melodic patterns in Mendelssohn's Scherzo in E minor, Op. 16.

The undulating movement discussed must be regarded as one of the most valuable and important in piano technique in preserving freedom and suppleness, and in avoiding rigidity. It combines with both finger-work and hand-staccato, and it is an auxiliary help in controlling rhythmic accentuation.

It can be mentioned in this chapter that staccato can also be produced, and is occasionally appropriate when, with the fingers in contact with the keys, downward impetus is supplied by the arm; this is allowed to result in a quick up-lift of the hand, wrist and fore-arm; from this up-lift the hand falls at once for the fingers to prepare silently the next notes to be played. The freedom and suppleness of the wrist and hand must be preserved in this 'rebound':

One sometimes sees attempts made to play very quiet staccato passages with fore-arm movement and a rigid wrist; this is to attempt a delicate judgment of tone using a relatively long and heavy tool. Control can so much more easily be achieved using a small hand movement from the wrist and with the fingers rising only fractionally above the key-surface. Incidentally, it should be borne in mind that many slow-moving notes and chords that may be marked staccato by the composer will not, in fact, be played with a staccato touch at all; the nature of the passage will determine the touch-form to be used, and the staccato sign refers to quick damping. Staccato shortens the length of a sound; it is not necessarily a touch. The example given employs fore-arm and wrist; each chord is prepared in advance on the key-surface.

## Fore-arm martellato action

Fore-arm-staccato will be assumed in heavy octaves and similar passages of chords of a martellato staccato character. The brilliant octave passages in the Tchaikovsky B flat minor Concerto

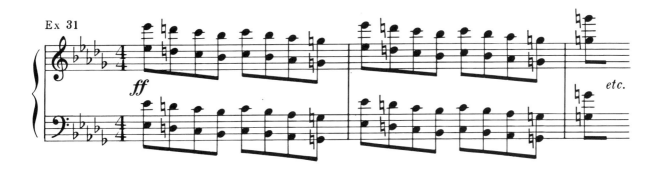

and in such works as the Chopin Third Scherzo and the Liszt B minor Sonata, call for this type of touch. It is essentially a percussive touch and it is normally restricted to forte and fortissimo passages. In appearance this is easily the most spectacular of the various touches used by pianists, and one recalls the extraordinary brilliance of Horowitz using this kind of touch in rapid octaves, and also the obvious enjoyment and gusto of Artur Rubinstein (in his younger days) lifting his hands and arms up to shoulder height in playing his favourite encore – *The Ritual Fire Dance* by de Falla – though this latter movement became something akin to a whole-arm-staccato.

As perhaps the most strenuous and tiring of touches it may be well to recommend that extended passages of this nature should not be practised to the point of exhaustion; they should be practised in relatively short spells, turning for relief to passages of a different nature that may require attention before returning to the heavy fore-arm passages for another short spell. Experiment has proved that for fortissimo octaves and for martellato passages such as occur on the final page of the Tchaikovsky First Concerto more power is available from a slightly higher base, therefore – do not crouch with rounded shoulders!

Ex 32

With a rapidly moving key- and piano-action for the required fortissimo, the 'sound-point' comes well before the key has reached the base (or key-bed), therefore great firmness is required on the surface of the key for this type of touch, but the forcefulness should not extend to the key-bed. It is interesting to reflect that rapidity in such fortissimo octaves is only possible because tone is produced early in the depressing of the keys; the speed of the octaves would be much retarded if it were necessary to press the blow home into the key-bed.

In the learning of chord passages that call for crisp percussive treatment (typical examples will be found in Prokofiev's Third Piano Concerto) it is obvious that the hand and fingers must be 'shaped' in advance if the hand is to drop directly into the keys from any degree of height.

Piano Concerto No. 3, 1st movement                                   Prokofiev

Ex 33

Piano Concerto No. 3, 3rd movement                                   Prokofiev

Ex 34

To train the hand to shape itself for each chord or hand-group, this training should first be done by placing the fingers in the required positions on the surface of the keys; later, as proficiency is gained, this shaping must be accomplished by visualising the positions of the fingers whilst the hand is above the keys and still in the act of falling. At the moment of contact the fingers will consciously grip the keys firmly; this will require precise timing.

The ear must be the judge of the degree of percussion in the touch that is aurally and artistically permissible: physically the more complete the fixation of the wrist the more hammer-like will be the blow and the harsher the tone. In moderating the degree of percussion there should be some elasticity of wrist in making contact with the keys, though the energy for tone-production in this type of touch will clearly emanate from the fore-arm.

## Rotary movement

If a finger of one hand be placed on the point of the opposite elbow joint it is possible to feel that the fore-arm can be rotated without movement of the upper arm. This rotary movement is an integral part of piano-playing as the fingers could not be placed with all the tips touching the keys without some rotary adjustment; e.g. with the arm swinging loosely at the side, lift the hand on to a table and note that it will fall on the outer (fifth finger) side of the hand; a movement, of which one is barely conscious, is necessary to bring all the fingers in contact with the surface. Rotary adjustments and stresses (mostly invisible) are taking place constantly in playing the piano. (Matthay has dealt well with this in his book *The Visible and the Invisible in Piano-forte Technique*.) It should be noted that fore-arm rotation is, strictly speaking, not an elbow-joint movement: it is, in fact, controlled by articulation of the radio-ulnar joint.

Of the conscious and visible applications of the rotary principle, such passages as tremolos will be assisted by it; almost any kind of passage where notes move in alternate directions (lower – higher) may receive energy assistance from rotation, but though rotary action is capable of considerable force, it does not substitute for crisp, firm finger-work.

Ex 35

Strong finger-action can however, legitimately receive useful and welcome auxiliary aid from rotary movement in such works as Chopin's Etude in A minor, Op. 25, No. 11.

Ex 36
Allegro con brio

In this latter example, starting at the *Allegro con brio* (fifth bar of the Etude) the right arm is extended to reach the highest octave of the keyboard; in this position there is a degree of rotation of the upper-arm, but as the passage falls lower in pitch and the extended arm, in consequence, gradually comes closer to the side of the body, so the upper-arm movement is reduced.

Rotary action is also called upon to help in giving emphasis to the upper or lower of two notes sounded together; to give greater speed to the note which requires prominence, the hand (which in preparation is turned slightly away from the note to be accented) turns in rotation towards this note, whilst the finger concerned will be muscularly braced to overcome the resistance of the key when imparting extra speed.

## Lateral freedom

The above term does not mean merely the necessary horizontal adjustment to cover, say, a four-octave scale, but primarily the conscious use of the capacity of the hand to turn sideways from the wrist combined with the ability of the fore-arm also to move from left to right and back again. The application of this movement becomes a necessity in many broken-chord accompanying figures which exceed the stretch of the hand (a type of formula frequently used by the romantic composers, e.g. Chopin in his Etude in A flat, Op. 25, No. 1).

In cultivating this action it is recommended to begin with a three-note figure (L. H. root, fifth and tenth of any chord). The third finger will be used as a pivot; the upper-arm will remain largely relaxed, moving very little, whilst the fore-arm moves freely left and right and in so doing it pulls the wrist left and right also. Meanwhile the pivot finger remains firmly in contact with the key. The fifth finger and thumb stretch in turn from the pivot finger to the outer notes which may be beyond their direct stretch. This exercise may also be extended to the root, sixth and eleventh intervals, using the second finger as pivot.

In executing this exercise the amount of lateral movement necessary is determined by (1) the need for the fifth finger to point as nearly as possible straight into the key from the tip to the second joint, and (2) for the thumb in its turn to point its nail-phalange directly into the key. The object of this is to prevent those fingers which are stretching out from falling diagonally across the white keys with the consequent risk of splitting notes. The finger-position will however be reversed if playing with an extended hand-position on black keys, when it becomes advisable for thumb and fifth finger to fall somewhat obliquely across the keys to which they will be stretching. It is estimated that the majority of accidentally 'split' notes which occur in otherwise accurate performances are due to imperfect adjustment for the lateral distances which must be covered; thus arises the necessity to realize and to appreciate the importance of such lateral adjustments when preparing works for performance. It will incidentally be realized that lateral movement in itself is not a touch but is used in combination with finger-action and (generally) a degree of rotary movement.

In the further development of lateral freedom Chopin's Etude in C major, Op. 10, No. 1, presents special problems.

In this study lateral extensions, in which the hand is stretched, alternate with contractions to small intervals between the fifth finger and thumb whilst the broken-chords are rising and falling continuously (mostly over four octaves). A further problem arises with the change of direction on reaching the top octave, where there should be an adjustment of the angle at which the hand and fore-arm are held relative to the keyboard; at this moment added impetus will be given to the start of the downward-moving notes with a swing of the elbow. This swing must be controlled so as not to disturb the required evenness of tone. Preparation for this study should be made by first adapting the physical movements required to easier and less stretched positions, as in the example given here:

It cannot be recommended too strongly that it is always a sound policy – and good common sense – to learn any difficult physical movement in the easiest available form. Analyse the difficulty as it is written in the work to be studied; ascertain precisely what it is that is awkward, then invent an easier formula for overcoming the fundamental difficulty of physical movement or co-ordination, transposing to an easier key, if necessary. This approach should be one of the cardinal maxims and essential principles of good practice.

In considering lateral freedom it may be well to suggest that a feeling for the geography of the keyboard (judging the distance apart of extended musical intervals) should be cultivated, by combining such lateral leaping intervals with hand-staccato and also with fore-arm-staccato. A first exercise may be to play single notes an octave apart, using staccato touch and employing second and fifth fingers; make a scale of this in C major, and when adept at it close the eyes and repeat each degree of the scale until a 'feeling' for the distance involved has been comfortably mastered. Follow this with a similar type of exercise but in thirds an octave apart – such as C and E played with the thumb and first finger, jumping to the same notes but an octave above, played by the fourth and fifth fingers.

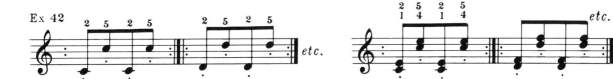

24

Make a scale of this, repeating each degree of the scale as may be necessary. Do this also with the eyes closed to develop further the feeling for the distance. Other exercises on these lines but of a more difficult pattern will suggest themselves to the advanced student.

## Use of the right pedal

The sustaining (damper) pedal was first patented in 1783 but before that some of the early pianos were fitted with knee-levers to operate the dampers. The knee-levers could not be used with the facility of the true pedal, therefore we may conclude that it is possible to play most of the keyboard music written before the 1780s without use of the right pedal, though discreet use of the sustaining pedal in the older music (notably in slow-moving passages) will certainly enrich tone quality.

The sustaining pedal has two primary functions − one practical, the other artistic. The first function enables the player to sustain notes when the fingers have lifted from the keys: legato can therefore be effected which would not otherwise be possible with the fingers alone. The other function comes about when, by lifting the dampers from the strings, all the strings of the instrument are free to vibrate, and those that are in the same harmonic series as any chord that is struck will influence tonal quality very considerably with their sympathetic vibration. Thus a pianist with an acute ear for tonal qualities will be making constant use of the right pedal to enrich the sounds which he is producing with his touch.

Haydn and Beethoven were the first two composers to realize the potentialities of the right pedal in producing special effects; Haydn in his C major (*English*) Sonata, Hob. 50, twice marks 'open Pedal' producing an atmospheric effect which must have been thought revolutionary,

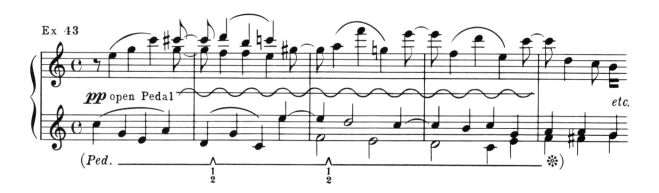

and Beethoven frequently marks in his manuscripts the use of pedal for special effects (one such is in the holding of background chords for the recitatives in Sonata, Op. 31, No. 2 in D minor).

Whilst a composer's marking of pedal for a special effect should never be ignored, the development of piano tone from the time of Haydn and Beethoven to the concert grands of today may on occasion justify some modification being made, and in the example quoted above (the recitatives in Op. 31, No. 2) many pianists prefer to hold down the quietly played notes of the L.H. chords of the sixth throughout each recitative whilst changing pedal at discretion. In considering the use of the pedal for enrichment of tone and for special effects the older Rubinstein (Anton) described the pedal as the 'soul of the piano', and its possibilities in adding warmth of tone (where appropriate) are endless.

The different ways in which a pianist may use the pedal are as follows:

*Legato pedalling* The foot will lift precisely as a new sound is heard, and will be re-depressed as soon as the ear notes that the previous sound is completely damped. The foot will therefore go down well after a note or chord has been played. As the foot goes down between the playing of notes it is sometimes called 'syncopated pedalling'.

*'Direct' pedalling* (This is not a universally acknowledged name for it.) The foot goes down as the note is played, with the object of enriching tone. It must be noted that as the damping of strings is not effected instantaneously (and there is therefore some time-lag) 'direct' pedalling can only be used for chords which are separated by rests or are staccato; otherwise there would be some residue of a previous sound to blur the effect.

*Half-pedalling* (A bad name for it, as the foot does in fact execute a complete lift.) The right-foot movement in 'half-pedalling' is precisely the same as in legato pedalling but is much speeded up: the foot lifts fully but is re-depressed (fully) immediately. The object is to sustain bass notes whilst clearing upper tones – taking advantage of the fact that the long bass strings of a piano take longer to damp than the shorter strings of higher-pitched notes.

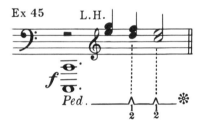

Try experimenting with very quick lifting and instant re-depressing of a firmly-struck bass note; and contrast this with the damping of notes in the treble clef! Note that no dampers are supplied to the top octave and a half, as the short strings of this high pitch have very little sustaining value.

*Half-damping* This is a matter of finding that point in the partial lifting (or depressing) of the dampers at which they, the dampers, are lightly touching the strings without resting on them with any pressure. An unique and curious tone quality can be produced, but as the dampers on many pianos are not always evenly adjusted or evenly worn it is a somewhat unreliable effect; moreover it is often difficult, when playing, to find on a strange piano just that point in the pressing-down of the pedal-lever which controls the dampers in the required position for the half-damping effect.

*'Flutter' or vibrato pedalling* Lifting the pedal rapidly up and down to secure quick reduction of tone that has been produced; or to secure an atmospheric effect of partial damping when that may be called for, not infrequently, in the works of Debussy and other more recent composers. This rapid up and down movement of the foot (always with the heel firmly resting on the ground) need not always be a complete release of the pedal to the top of its movement; and in this respect 'flutter' pedalling may well justifiably become a rapid alternation of 'on' and 'off' half-dampings (see above). As ever, the movement of the foot will be governed by the ears.

26

When considering the two main functions of the pedal, it is as well occasionally to remind ourselves that they cannot be separated. We may be pedalling for the purely practical purpose of effecting a legato which the fingers alone cannot encompass, but we also inevitably have the benefit of the sympathetic resonance of unstruck strings vibrating; we should aim to maintain a consistent quality of tone, and not be content with some notes rich with pedal and others relatively 'dry' within the same phrase.

For the advanced player who knows well what he is doing, there will be occasions when a deliberate slight overlap in legato pedalling can be effective. The overlap must not be longer than just to cover the tone-production of the next chord. Examples are found in the theme of the second movement of Beethoven's *Appassionata* Sonata

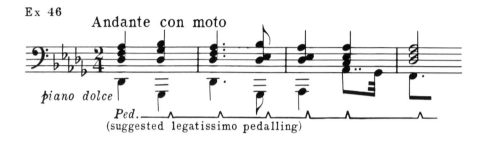

and in chords of the first two statements in his Fourth Concerto, second movement.

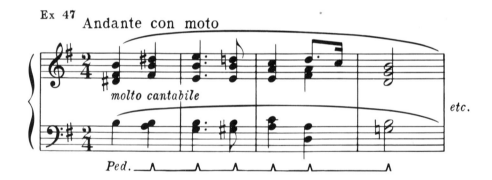

The desired effect is to achieve a legatissimo that aims to mask the sound of the hammers striking the strings (similar to that already described for legatissimo finger-work in cantabile passages).

Reference is sometimes made to 'quarter-pedalling', etc. (see Neuhaus's book *The Art of Pianoforte Playing*). Simple observation of the movement of the dampers caused by pressing-down and releasing the right pedal shows that unless the pedal-lever is allowed to rise virtually to the top, the dampers will come nearer to the strings but will not actually touch them; obviously no damping at all takes place unless contact is made. Experiment and attentive listening will show if a complete lift of pedal is necessary for half-pedalling or if some degree of partial lift suffices to produce the desired effect.

A disturbing habit is that of manipulating the pedals noisily. The right foot, which is frequently called upon to make rapid 'changing' movements, is the offender normally. The player should be made aware of the unpleasant clanging of the pedal-lever and/or the thud of the dampers being allowed to fall on the strings too rapidly, and he should practise the use of the pedal at various speeds until this can be managed without either mechanical or damper noise. There should be no sounding of notes whilst this foot-technique is being acquired. Note that a slower lift can be used to damp more gradually ('flutter' pedalling can also control the speed of damping).

## Una corda

The term *una corda* is misleading as it is a very long time since the action of the 'soft' pedal on grand pianos was modified so that the keyboard and action of the piano, in moving, now causes the hammers to strike two strings of the three-per-note which cover most of the compass of the instrument. The effect of the true *una corda* was presumably found too drastic though in a few of Beethoven's scores one finds *due corde e poi una corda*, implying that Beethoven found an artistic use for the left pedal to be partly depressed as well as fully depressed.

In striking two strings instead of three, the tone produced (and amplified by the sound-board) is, of course, reduced; but most pianists would agree that the more important difference in tone is caused by the hammers hitting the strings on a less-used (and therefore softer) part of the felt hammer-heads. The softer felt sets up less strong overtones (or upper partials) and there is a considerable difference in quality of tone (as distinct from quantity); this is, in fact, the *only* tonal difference caused by the *una corda* in the lower part of the compass where, in the extreme bass there is only one string per note and, above that pitch, for approximately one and a half octaves, two strings per note. Another lesser influence is the sympathetic vibration of the string which is not struck. These factors rightly suggest to the player that if his quality is to be consistent for a given passage, the left pedal will be used throughout that passage without lifting, in order to give consistency of tone-colour. As to the sheer reduction of sound that is caused, the pianist with a good control of touch should be able to produce the softest of pianissimos without the use of the *una corda*, but few would deny that if confronted with a bright-toned piano in a resonant auditorium they would unhesitatingly use the *una corda* for the purpose of producing softer tones where necessary. Nevertheless, the *una corda* should be used sparingly, and primarily in order to give different tone-colour to passages of different texture or in different key.

It remains to mention that on upright pianos (continental name: 'pianinos') the effect of the left pedal is to bring the hammers closer to the strings, which successfully reduces the speed at which they strike the strings, thereby reducing tone; unfortunately there is no difference in the quality of the tone whether with or without the 'soft' pedal of the upright.

On the larger Steinway pianos and on many American pianos there is a third (middle) pedal. This is sometimes known as the 'sostenente' pedal and it is selective. It controls a device which holds back any dampers which are not resting on the strings when this third pedal is depressed. This permits such strings to continue vibrating, but has no effect on the rest. If, for example, an octave in the bass is struck and the middle pedal depressed whilst the keys concerned are still held down, the bass octave will continue to sound but any notes sounded afterwards will remain clear of pedal. It is customary to operate the 'sostenente' with the left foot, leaving the right foot to its normal duties. The idea of the 'sostenente' is admirable but in practice there are not many occasions when it can effectively be called upon. To a great extent it duplicates the function of half-pedalling.

## Summary

This analysis of physical movements and of pedalling that go to the making of a comprehensive technique has no pretensions to constituting a 'Method'. That great teacher of the past, Leschetizky, insisted that he had no method, holding firmly that each pupil according to his character and personality needed a different approach.

Technique must not be regarded as more than a means to an end; it should help one to achieve the maximum of artistic effect with the minimum of effort. Let Busoni have the last word in saying: 'Technique in the truer sense has its seat in the brain.'

CHAPTER III

# More technical matters, with some comments on aural training

## The aural approach

In the development of piano technique it is clear that an alert mental awareness of what is appropriate and of what is required is vital if the player is to perform intelligently and accurately; we shall also find that balanced and sensitive interpretations require that one should be conscious of style, have an intellectual grasp of structure and be responsive to any emotional demands. Before considering such matters it must however be stressed that a young musician's thoughts must also be directed to realize the importance of aural awareness and aural imagination, needing training of the ear up to a high standard.

From the earliest stages the act of touch and the consequent tone-production must be governed by the demand of the ear for tone of a certain strength, balance and quality. A course in aural training should lead to the immediate recognition of intervals and cadences, together with the ability to isolate individual notes of chords and, as a logical development of this last requirement, the capacity to follow independent parts (or 'voices') in contrapuntal music. Ear training must also include the development of a precise rhythmic sense and the ability to maintain a steady, even pulse and tempo over a long period—the student can discipline himself by beating time to first-class recorded performances (preferably of classical chamber and orchestral music). It is also necessary to cultivate a quick response to changing rhythmic patterns within a work; it is, for instance, surprising how frequently even advanced students will alter the pulse-rate of the main beat when sub-divisions change from duplets to triplets, or from triplets to quadruplets, or vice versa. A course of eurhythmics from an early age will help enormously in developing the rhythmic sense.

The intelligent and sensitive teacher will also make his pupils aware of any aural virtues that are of special value to the pianist, such as: developing an acute ear for balance of sound, showing how the character of a chord can be altered by accentuation of different notes of that chord; and, arising from such control of tone, acquiring the ability to play and to listen for tones of varied intensity from each hand (as often in melody and accompaniment); similarly, to be able to listen to tones of contrasted strength when played by the same hand, as is often required in part-playing.

In the matter of intonation the pianist is of course normally dependent on the professional tuner, but with tonal quality the teacher will endeavour to cultivate his pupils' appreciation of beauty of sound. This implies that the teacher will frequently play contrasted (and technically efficient!) examples on which the pupil will be required to differentiate and criticize. The student should also often be asked to criticize his own tone and playing, hoping thus to encourage a faculty for attentive listening whilst fostering an aptitude for self-criticism. (It may, at this juncture, be well to stress the important difference between 'listening' – giving one's whole attention to something that is heard, and 'hearing' which implies being conscious of a sound without necessarily paying heed to it. The musician, being trained to 'listen', generally has a hearty dislike of background 'music').

The teacher should also stimulate the student imaginatively to tonal awareness (among other aspects of artistic development) in such ways as in showing that many of Mozart's melodic lines in his piano works seem to demand beautiful singing (though they may exceed the range of the voice), and that much of Beethoven's piano music asks for instrumental and, at times, orchestral sounds. In addition, the aspiring pianist should not confine himself to listening only to other pianists, however distinguished, but should seek opportunities to hear orchestral and chamber music, and to listen to eminent singers and virtuosi on other instruments, noting and appreciating the sheer beauty and quality of different kinds of sounds.

Finally, one of the aims of thorough aural training will be to enable the musician to hear what he sees, i.e. to imagine accurately, away from an instrument, the sound of what his eyes perceive in a musical score; he will in consequence then be able to 'think' through a work in silence, planning an interpretation that is not influenced by temporary technical difficulties.

## Processes in the development of technical facility

Turning now to keyboard matters: when one considers the practical application of the principles and movements involved in piano technique account must be taken of the muscular and nervous aspects. As implied by Busoni, in his already quoted statement that 'technique . . . has its seat in the brain', the brain conceives and instigates physical movement, and the nervous system responds to impulses from the brain; the nerves convey such impulses to the muscles concerned which, in turn, control the physical movements of arms, wrists, hands and fingers.

The physical movements concerned in playing, say, five-finger exercises will at first be deliberately controlled in detail at a slow pace; as facility is gained, the notes and the movements to which they give rise will eventually be 'thought' in groups. Recognition of the need to think and to play in groups of notes is necessary if any degree of fluency is to be achieved both in (i) reading musical notation and (ii) developing any technical dexterity. The comparison may be made with a child's learning of a language in which, as soon as possible, the laborious stage of spelling-out the simplest and shortest of words letter by letter should be left behind; a normal child quickly learns to see, and to understand, short words as a whole in their different, composite shapes, and the process should develop in due course to the comprehension of an ever-wider vocabulary, read silently or aloud at the speed of fluent adult reading. Similarly in music, one aims to get quickly past the elementary stage of reading individual notes, and to read notes in simple uncomplicated groups which are the equivalent of short words in a language. When simple note-groups can be grasped as a whole and imagined aurally as composite sounds, the effort must be made to build two or more such groups into short phrases (musical sentences). From this beginning, fluent reading of notation should be developed.

It is also necessary to think in groups and to cultivate quick physical reaction to such groups in order to acquire finger agility and general technical fluency. It must be accepted that, inevitably and unavoidably, instrumental practice requires constant and patient repetition of passages. The repetitions result in due course in the physical movements concerned becoming acquired or conditioned reflex actions responding almost automatically to the shapes and the technical demands of the notes. It will be realized that conditioned reflex actions of this nature are of the greatest value to the player; they will become faster than the quickest mind can consciously direct them. Playing with any degree of speed is therefore governed by the response and swiftness of one's conditioned reflexes.

The simplest kind of example will be a five-finger group such as:

In such a grouping, played at a fast pace, the individual actions of fingers are such conditioned reflex actions. It should be noted that the ear must nevertheless be alert to detect any note that is uneven or missing, and if such a defect should occur the passage should temporarily be repeated more slowly until the unevenness is overcome.

Further thought on this matter of acquiring velocity in playing quick passage-work, sometimes with both hands occupied with such rapid notes (as in the Coda of Chopin's Fourth Ballade and many other similar examples) convinces one that it is indeed impossible to think fast enough to direct consciously each finger at the required tempo. Instead, one 'thinks' in groups that may be primarily melodic or harmonic, or a combination of the two, and the physical response of playing the notes within the groups will of necessity be by acquired reflex action.

Ballade in F minor, Op. 52      Chopin

Ex 49   Agitato

The training towards such group-thinking and reflex action is therefore vital in developing velocity, accuracy and control of technique. The goal should be to strive to develop rapid nervous and muscular responses and control of the marvellous human mechanism concerned.

## Scales

The fingering of scales in groups provides the most important single principle of fingering. This principle is that every scale, over the compass of one octave, will be conveniently fingered in two groups; certain keys share the fingering that is normally taken for C major (1 2 3, 1 2 3 4, for R.H. rising and L.H. falling) but the general principle when black keys are involved is that the thumb will commence a group by being placed on the first white key after a black key or group of black keys. (This also applies to R.H. rising and L.H. falling, but the principle may of course also be expressed in reverse form, i.e. thumb on last white key before a black key, R.H. falling and L.H. rising.) There is no 'mystique' about this placing of the thumb in relation to the black keys: it merely makes use of the fact that the black keys of the keyboard, though shorter, are raised above the white keys, and the fingers (well-rounded in position) which play on the black keys provide a slightly higher (and therefore easier) bridge under which to 'pass' the thumb. It should be made clear that this 'passing-under' commences at once as the thumb lifts from its last note, and the movement proceeds steadily and gradually, without jerk, until the thumb is ready for its next note which will be the interval of a fourth or fifth above. The thumb requires preliminary training to acquire suppleness and facility in its movement under the hand, and in making the independent vertical movement which is somewhat alien to its normal gripping or stretching action. In joining the hand-groups smoothly through this turning-under of the thumb there will be some lateral pivotting on the intervening fingers, with a tendency for the wrist and fore-arm to lead the way. It should be noted that in playing a descending scale in the R.H. (L.H. rising) the action will be considerably different: in this case the turning of third or fourth fingers over the thumb receives some assistance from rotary action of the fore-arm; it is advisable that in turning over the thumb the fingers will all be placed as soon as possible over the keys which they are next to play – thus always being prepared over their keys slightly in advance. Do not permit fingers that are not playing to lose their rounded position; no finger should straighten and point into the air. Incidentally, it is interesting to observe that the 'perfect' position for the fingers is found with the following notes

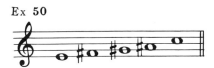

Ex 50

and that the two keys which provide the most comfortable positions for the fingers and the easiest turn-under points are B major for the R.H. and D flat major for the L.H.; B major is said to have been the first key which Chopin habitually taught to his pupils.

It is incidentally a curious inconsistency with scale-manuals (and with general teaching practice) to ignore the above principle governing the placing of the thumb on the first white key following a black key, in the case of the left hand in the keys of F major, G major, D major and A major which are invariably given the C major fingering of 5 4 3 2 1 etc. Consistency with regard to the principle stated would place the thumb differently in each case. There is the additional inconsistency in that the descending forms of D major and of B in the relative minor, which consist of precisely the same notes, are given entirely different fingerings:

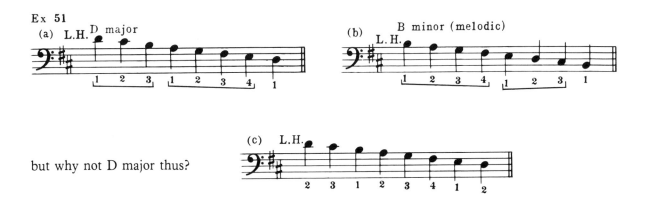

Ex 51
(a) L.H. D major

(b) B minor (melodic)
L.H.

but why not D major thus?

(c) L.H.

which would certainly suit D major much better when for instance played a sixth apart:

(d) R.H.

L.H.

Adherence to a consistent principle of fingering is recommended. (A responsible examining body will normally accept any practical and systematic fingering which produces a good result.) May it be suggested that if an intelligent pupil has grasped (a) the construction of major and minor scales and (b) the principle of fingering involved, the use of a scale-manual is superfluous and may advantageously be replaced by requiring the pupil to write out for himself the various scales, as they are learnt, with the appropriate fingerings?

The value of scale and arpeggio playing is sometimes questioned, and it is well to be clear why they are both indispensable as a foundation for technique. It must however be stated that well-chosen exercises are also necessary for the cultivation of independence, freedom and suppleness of movement of all the fingers. Among the many good books of exercises Brahms' excellent *51 Uebungen* and Hanon's *The Virtuoso Pianist* may be recommended. The resourceful teacher will choose an appropriate selection of exercises from such books (not necessarily starting with No. 1) and should invent others suggested by actual difficulties encountered in the works of the great masters. The student should be given a simple modulating plan and should practise such exercises in all keys (taking perhaps three or four keys per day for each exercise) – and not always starting with C major! Playing in different keys also provides good elementary practice in transposition.

In the teaching and learning of scales both teacher and pupil should be aware of the special value or purpose of scales at different stages of development. The relative beginner will learn scales primarily (i) to acquire a knowledge of keys and (ii) to learn the first principles of fingering (as explained above). The scales will be played at first with hands separately at slow pace, firmly and evenly. When some facility has been attained, the hands will be played together, perhaps at first in contrary motion over one octave, in those keys in which the hands share a common fingering; the asymmetric fingering of similar motion scales is generally found more difficult. This stage should be mastered as quickly as possible.

The second stage, which may be expected to last over a longer period, will aim to combine increasing fluency with absolute precision in striking the notes of each hand simultaneously. Scales with the hands playing a third, a sixth and a tenth apart will present problems in the matter of keeping the hands well together at an even distance apart. During this stage scales will be played with varied rhythmic groupings (four notes and eight notes to the group over a compass of four octaves and with three notes and six notes to the group over a compass of three octaves); also in varied rhythms and with contrasting touches (e.g. legato for R.H. and staccato for L.H., etc.). When playing with separate hands, speeds up to approximately ♩ = 132 for four sixteenth notes may be attempted, at the discretion of the teacher. At any sign of unevenness the tempo should be temporarily reduced.

In the final stage, extending to the standard of the concert pianist, the greatest possible degree of control should be the aim. Tempi up to prestissimo, and with different strengths of tone (also with crescendo and diminuendo) must be mastered. It will be presumed that at this stage the striking of the hands together with precision will present no further difficulty; therefore it is no paradox that in advanced playing the greatest benefit will be found in practising scales with hands separately; the possible weakness of a finger in one hand must not be covered or masked by the strength of a finger in the other hand striking a note an octave apart at the same moment. Acute and concentrated listening to each hand separately as well as to hands together is vitally necessary to ensure that tonal and rhythmic evenness is under perfect control at all speeds.

Naturally there will be overlapping of such different stages but, in general, these divisions hold. It may be remarked that the teacher and pupils alike often seem to have a conviction that once scales can be played with hands together there is no further benefit to be obtained from continuing to play them with hands separately. Nothing could be more mistaken! And the playing of scales with separate hands, in addition to hands together, should be insisted on at all stages.

It will be realized that varying forms of scale and arpeggio passages provide the majority of technical difficulties throughout the classical repertoire, and to have a fluent mastery of scales in all keys is to be equipped in advance to deal with such difficulties when they are encountered. In recommending strongly that scales will be practised with hands separately up to the highest possible standard, it should be noted that there are in fact relatively few passages in piano literature in which both hands are simultaneously occupied with scale playing. There are a few such instances in concertos when 'doubled' scales may be heard against orchestral themes or harmonies, and there are short passages of scales with hands together at the ends of several of Chopin's works, but these instances are rare compared with the countless examples of single-handed passage-work, founded on scales and arpeggios standing separately exposed.

## Double-thirds scales (so called even when playing hands separately!)

Before embarking on the playing of double-thirds scales some preliminary exercises will be necessary, primarily to ensure that both notes of the thirds are sounded precisely together. It will be found that when proceeding for instance from $\frac{4}{2}$ to $\frac{5}{3}$ that the third finger, being longer than the fifth, has an annoying tendency to sound first unless a slight adjustment of hand position is made to compensate for the relative shortness of the fifth finger. The following exercises may be found useful:

In the fingering of double-thirds major scales the basic principle of using two groups of fingers to cover the compass of one octave is in general preferable to the three-group system.

The complete formula for double thirds in major keys is:

Two-group fingering
{
R.H.    3 4 5 2 3 4 5    applying to C, G, D, A and E
       1 2 3, 1 1 2 3,

L.H.    3 2 1 3 2 1 1
      5 4 3, 5 4 3 2,    applying to C, G, D and A
}

The three-group system would in each case take two short groups:

3 4 3 4    instead of    2 3 4 5   ; the group    3 4 5    remains unchanged
1 2, 1 2,             1 1, 2 3,            1 2 3,
(reverse for L.H.)

Fingering for keys with flats (F, B flat, E flat and A flat): as with single-note scales, they will be played (R.H. descending, L.H. ascending) with the thumb on the last white key before a black key or group of black keys. The thumb will always be taken three times in each octave, and the rule with regard to the placing of the thumb implies that some keys will start with incomplete finger-groups.

The keys of B major, F sharp (G flat) major and C sharp (D flat) major each contain only two white keys: in these three keys the thumb will be played on the two white keys and on F sharp in each case in the R.H., and on A sharp in each case in the L.H.

On the basis of the above formula the student should write out and finger each scale for himself as with single-note scales; the use of a scale-manual is unnecessary.

When playing double-thirds legato it is not possible to join both notes of the thirds smoothly when connecting the finger groups, nor when playing the thumb on two consecutive notes. The illusion of legato must be created by securing the smoothest possible progression between the upper notes of the

R.H. when rising, and the lower notes of the L.H. when falling; to connect the groups in these cases it will be found helpful to point the hand outwards, enabling the longer second or third fingers to play over the fifth finger to make the legato join. This is a difficult movement to accomplish, and the following exercise will provide a preparation for it:

The descending form of the R.H. (L.H. ascending) is easier as the hand turns over the thumb in connecting the groups of fingers. In the double-thumb position it will be obvious that the fingers playing simultaneously with the thumb provide the necessary legato.

The above principles for fingering and hand position also hold good for double thirds in minor keys, but in some harmonic minors it will be found that the thumb would fall consecutively on keys an augmented second apart; in such cases it may be more convenient to take the two short groups of the three-group system to avoid the thumb jumping, as in G sharp minor, from F double-sharp (enharmonically G natural) to E. (*cf.* Chopin's Etude in G sharp minor, Op.25, No.6.)

## Chromatic scales

Several fingerings are possible for chromatic single-note scales; these are not entirely a matter of personal preference, but should be used for different speeds and different degrees of tone. Thus: it is usual to teach the following fingering first: (i) (starting on D from which note the R.H. may be read ascending and the L.H. descending) 1 3 1 2 3 1 3 1 3 1 2 3. Here only the strongest fingers of the hand are used, but the thumb has to turn under the hand five times in each octave which reduces the speed of progression, therefore in advanced playing this fingering is regarded as suitable only for firm, forte passages of no great velocity. (ii) A faster fingering (also imagine starting on D for the same reason that the hands can be read in reverse): 1̲ 2̲ 3̲, 1̲ 2̲ 3̲ 4̲, 1̲ 2̲ 3̲, 1̲ 2̲ 3̲ 4̲, 1̲ 2̲ 3̲, 1̲ 2̲ 3̲ 4̲, 1̲ 2̲ 3̲. This fingering recurs only every two octaves and within this compass it alternates between two finger groups, allowing the thumb at least two intervening notes to accomplish its turn-under; it will often be used for more rapid passages of a possibly lighter nature. (iii) A third fingering covers the compass of one octave in three groups:

1 2 3 1 2 3 4 1 2 3 4 5 and can be learnt as starting on E (R.H. rising) and C (L.H. falling). (It can also be practised starting on C (R.H. rising) and E (L.H. falling), the order of fingering being in this case: 1 2 3 4 1 2 3 1 2 3 4 5.) It is sometimes called 'the Liszt fingering', as Liszt is known to have used it. Passages combining extreme speed with 'leggierissimo' will find a use for it; an example can be found in the untimed rising chromatic scale in the fourth Beethoven Concerto (bar 159, third movement). (iv) Still another fingering is found in scale manuals: 1 3 1 2 3 1 2 3 4 1. This is inclined to be uneven rhythmically unless great care is taken: by employing 1 3 1 it requires the thumb to turn under with only one intervening finger (with implied limitation of speed) whilst it shares with fingering No. (ii) the grouping 1 2 3 1 2 3 4 which permits greater rapidity. (N.B. Certain notes have been mentioned above for convenience in commencing the groups; after learning first by beginning on these notes one should be able to start anywhere.)

Ex. 55

Groupings are unchanged
in reverse direction

A few hints may be useful on the playing of chromatic minor thirds. The preliminary practice for these will be to acquire facility playing first the upper notes alone, then the lower notes also separately (in each case with the appropriate fingering as for the complete minor thirds). The recommended fingering for chromatic minor thirds is:

Ex 56

The figures for fingering are given for R.H.; for L.H. the same groupings apply, but read: $\frac{345}{121} = \frac{121}{345}$
etc.

The sliding of the second finger causes adjustments to be made in the fingering on reversing direction. This sliding needs considerable control but is more legato and can be faster than the double-thumb fingering which is often advocated as an alternative.

## Octave technique

The approach to detached octaves will be different according to the amount of tone required but in all cases the best preliminary practice for octaves will be to repeat each degree of a scale several times in well-marked rhythmic patterns of threes, fours, fives and sixes. It is helpful to practise octave scales and other octave passages with thumb only and also with fifth finger only – as preparatory exercises.

When the tone is light, a hand-staccato touch will be used, with the auxiliary help of the undulating principle already described (pages 16-17). If the tone is to be forte or fortissimo the touch will be a martellato from the fore-arm, and accents for the first notes of the groups will have the assistance of energy from the upper-arm with consequent reaction felt by the shoulder. The thumb and fifth finger will be held firmly 'braced' and the shape of the hand will be something like a two-pronged fork.

A typical example of heavy detached octaves is found in Chopin's Third Scherzo in C sharp minor:

At first repeat each octave rhythmically at varying tempi, noting that the thumb and fifth finger will grip the keys firmly as the hand strikes and the fingers make contact. Then play the three octaves of the third bar and proceed without a break to the first note of the next bar (repeat this progression of four notes). Finally play and repeat the two bars together.

It is generally important to note the 'direction of travel' in octave passages: the octaves on the first page of the Liszt B minor Sonata supply an admirable example. The first descending triplet eighth-notes start on black keys and proceed to white keys, whilst the second set of triplet eighth-notes start with white keys and finish on black keys.

In the first case the fingers and hand will start well back on the black keys (towards the wood of the 'fall') and will move obliquely forward in descending on to the white keys. This oblique motion is reversed in the second example. The principle involved can advantageously be applied in many cases, as for example in the Chopin Polonaise in A flat: in the middle section of this work L.H. octaves begin in E major, and the movement of the hand executes a crescent-shaped pattern in playing the four notes, moving slightly forward for the black keys before returning to cover the white keys; when the passage slips down into E flat the shape of the crescent is reversed (as convex is to concave):

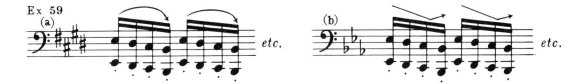

Scales and arpeggios in octaves should be a part of daily practice; arpeggios can be split into patterns of three or four notes, to be repeated: dominant and diminished sevenths should be included.

Legato octaves are best learnt through the practice and playing of the chromatic octave scale, when the fourth finger will be taken on the black keys. The Chopin Etude in B minor, Op. 25, No. 10, provides a magnificent example of legato octaves.

It will be understood that it is not possible to make truly legato a succession of octaves on white keys only. The fingers will keep as close to the keys as possible in such cases, sliding with no perceptible gap from note to note. If the hand is large enough, white-note octaves should always be taken with the hand well over the keys, not playing from the forward edge; the object of this will be to reduce to a minimum any movement of the hand forwards and backwards (in and out of the keys) in proceeding from white keys to black and back again. A further point with regard to octave-playing is that in placing the thumb on adjacent white and black keys, the nail-phalange of the thumb should point directly forward into the key in the case of white keys, and then played diagonally across a following black key: this is done to avoid the risk of 'splitting' white keys (and sounding two together) by playing across them, and in the case of the black keys to reduce the danger of slipping off the narrower black key. The practice of the following exercises should aim to make the bending and straightening of the thumb's nail-phalange automatic, until it becomes another acquired reflex responding to the circumstances:

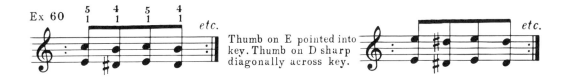

Thumb on E pointed into key. Thumb on D sharp diagonally across key.

Whilst legato octaves will, as stated above, be played with the use of the fourth finger on the black keys, brilliant staccato octaves are generally better keeping to the thumb and fifth finger on the black keys, thereby avoiding the slight change in the hand position which would be caused by the use of the fourth finger.

## Broken chords and arpeggios

Before embarking on arpeggios the student should cultivate a firm grasp of broken chords in order to acquire a feeling for the spacing of chords, being careful to avoid the use of the third finger in those chord positions where the use of the fourth finger is more natural and appropriate. The formulae for broken chords should be varied using the following two finger-patterns: (a) 1235, 1245 and (b) 1325, 1425. Pattern (a) implies notes in direct sequence, for which the player will find some lateral adjustment helpful; in pattern (b) with notes alternately rising and falling in pitch, the player will find that the fingers may receive assistance from a little fore-arm rotation.

38

The chief difficulty of arpeggios, as compared with scales, lies in the greater distance which the thumb has to move in turning-under to connect the hand groups. This problem is most acute and prominently displayed in the rising root positions from white keys in the R.H. and falling second inversions from white keys in the L.H. The thumb is in these cases faced with turning-under to cover the interval of a fourth, and it is not long enough to cover this distance without a compensating movement of the arm to assist it. This movement of the arm will certainly enable the thumb to join quite smoothly the hand groups concerned, but the arm-movement mentioned leaves the hand in a bad position to continue the arpeggio; in slow playing the recovery to a normal position can be accomplished without disturbing tone and rhythm, but in rapid arpeggios this becomes impossible, and an alternative method (or at least an adjustment) has to be sought. This adjustment will be such that the thumb does indeed turn under as far as possible (it will in fact be over the note that is a third above the last note played); there is then a controlled lateral shift of the hand to enable the thumb to cover the small remaining distance to reach the note that is a fourth above; the fingers remain in a normal position pointing into the keys, there is no change in the angle of the hand, and the second and third fingers are ready to continue the unbroken progress of the arpeggio. It may appear that there could be a momentary break in legato when the quick lateral adjustment is made but the damping of sound, which is progressively slower towards the bass, is not instantaneous on any piano, and as we are now concerned with the playing of quick arpeggios there is in fact no audible break whatever in the playing of the arpeggio. Exercises to overcome this very real difficulty will include:

It is scarcely necessary to mention that common chord arpeggios and their inversions should be played over four octaves in groups of four, and that dominant and diminished seventh arpeggios should be played over a compass of three octaves in groups of three, thereby avoiding the accent always falling on the same note and finger. Before leaving the question of the grouping and fingering of notes in arpeggios, attention must be drawn to Brahms' practice of implying four-note finger-groups for common chords, as well as for chords of the seventh. This grouping can on occasion help the rhythm when passages including four sixteenth-notes are involved; care needs to be taken to ensure that there is no audible break when proceeding from group to group. This grouping from thumb to fifth finger (and vice versa) can of course be applied to the works of other composers. Examples from Brahms are given below:

Rhapsody in E flat, Op. 119

Variations on a theme of Handel

# The development of trills

The first necessity for a trill is that each of the alternating fingers must cultivate an ability to strike, lift and to strike again with great rapidity. This implies that each finger should be individually trained on the following lines:

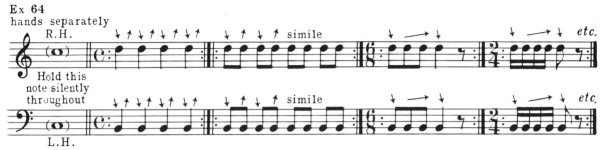

Ex 64
hands separately

Cultivate repetitions combined with undulating fore-arm and wrist movement. Use each pair of fingers (12; 23; 34; 45).

As it is all too easy for a repeating finger to tap on the surface of the key without producing a reliable tone, this exercise, as a preliminary, should be played with long slow notes and with a 'deep' touch and free arm movement assisting the playing of each note. The exercise will then be developed to increase gradually the speed of repetitions in strict rhythmic groupings (though the final result may be a 'free' trill without rhythmic sub-divisions). An undulating 'down-up' movement of the fore-arm (similarly as in hand-staccato repetitions of sixths, eighths, etc.) will be helpful. Each pair of consecutive fingers will be used, and only when independence and facility of each finger is considered adequate will the trill itself be attempted, with the assistance of a minimum of the undulating arm-movement. At first just one beat of the trills should be played, giving relaxation at the end of each group:

Ex 65

Only gradually should the length of the trills be extended, maintaining always the freedom of the undulatory arm-movement, falling into the first of a group, then rising gradually towards the end of the group. (It is, incidentally, a common fault to rise too soon.)

In addition to the above which are primarily finger trills, it will be necessary to cultivate trills with the assistance of fore-arm rotary action, as in tremolos. As rotary movement is at its maximum between thumb and fifth finger, as in tremolos of a sixth and octave, etc., so in the more restricted interval of a tone or semitone, any trill which has the auxiliary help of fore-arm rotation will be better played with alternate fingers (such as 1−3, 2−4 and 3−5), which permit more freedom of rotary movement than when using consecutive fingers. It will be realized that fore-arm rotation, which is not a touch form in itself, is on occasion a very useful source of extra power behind the fingers; it is therefore more likely to be called upon in music demanding the full resources of the modern concert grand.

One other form of trill needs to be taken into consideration, and this is a trill with a change of finger: 2 3 1 3 2 3 1 3 or 1 3 2 3 1 3 2 3, which is suitable for trills lasting several beats and requiring great velocity; a hint of the undulatory fore-arm and wrist movement described above is useful in playing this kind of trill. As the finger-change gives a four-note grouping it is musically and technically better to restrict this trill to passages in which multiples of four (i.e. thirty-second- and sixty-fourth-notes) are acceptable.

Trills of any considerable length (a bar or more) should generally be regarded as 'free' trills, i.e. trills without rhythmic sub-division; in the case of trills decorating short-value notes it is always wise to decide exactly how many notes can be musically and effectively fitted into the time available. If the tempo is slow a modest group of five notes, possibly with final 'turn' as suffix, may sound banal and feeble, but in general it is better to play a limited number of notes clearly than to attempt a greater number that may be untidy and which may, in the effort, interfere with the even flow of rhythm. In slow movements it is seldom appropriate to play a very fast trill; trills at the ends of Bach's Chromatic Fantasia and the *Andante* from the Italian Concerto require only a gentle alternation of notes.

It is not the function of this book to discuss ornamentation in detail, and generalizations must suffice. J.S. Bach's own table of ornaments which was written out for his 12 year old son W. Friedemann Bach must be taken as the authoritative source for that period (though the list is not complete).

From this list it will be gathered that trills will start on the upper auxiliary note, and in the case of the Baroque and Early Classical Periods there is no evidence of any exceptions to this principle in the writings of C.P.E. Bach or others of his contemporaries. Nevertheless there was surely never a 'rule' without exceptions, and in this case it would appear that too strict an adherence would sometimes cause consecutive (parallel) fifths – which would no doubt be anathema to J.S. Bach. Taste, supported by knowledge and common sense must be the arbiter. It is, incidentally to be emphasized that Bach in his 'Explication' gives the sign ⤳ as the true mordent, and ∿ as a 'trillo'. The current habit in many quarters of calling ∿ a mordent and ⤳ an inverted mordent is clearly contrary to the musical language of Bach and his contemporaries; it is deplored as leading to confusion and possibly to errors in performance, therefore it is urged that the teaching of ornamentation as part of the rudiments of music should conform to the customs of the period concerned. For a full discussion of ornamentation see Walter Emery's excellent book *Bach's Ornaments* (Novello) and also the relevant pages of C.P.E. Bach's *Essay on the True Art of Playing Keyboard Instruments* (Eulenburg Books, London). Two additional points should be mentioned in these brief comments on the subject: (i) it may be assumed that all ornaments in the time of Bach start on, and not before, the beat (a rare exception is the 'Nachschlag' or quick appoggiatura – which C.P.E. Bach disliked); (ii) that a change occurred in the last years of the eighteenth century with regard to the view taken of the sign ⁓ which, as we have seen, was in Bach's time understood to be a trill of four or more notes starting on the upper auxiliary. We find Beethoven using this ornament in the *Pathétique* Sonata, Op. 13, dating from 1798–9 and quite clearly intending a three-note ornament starting on the written note.

Beethoven also uses the same sign for similar effect a few years later in his Third Concerto in C minor (first movement);

and it is worth noting that Chopin used the same sign ⁓ in the third bar of his Ballade No. 3 in A flat where it is also intended as a three-note ornament.

This may be taken as a warning not to apply the customs and traditions of one period when dealing with music of another generation.

## Fingering

Scales were quoted as providing an introduction to the principles of fingering in teaching the importance of thinking in groups of notes (to be played by appropriate groups of fingers); this was coupled with the fact that when a lateral shift of hand position on the keyboard was necessary the thumb would be the linking finger. To this principle must be added the comment that in fingering any passage-work (which is generally derived from, or incorporates, some form of scale and arpeggio patterns) one needs to keep in mind the relative lengths of the fingers in relation to the black keys which are of course shorter than the white keys.

42

The normal position on the white keys is such that the tips of the well-rounded second, third and fourth fingers should just reach to the end (or base) of the black keys. From this position, if the thumb or fifth finger are to play on the black keys it is necessary to reach forward extending the arm; this disturbance to the arm-position in any kind of rapid passage makes tonal control difficult. It is often better therefore in single-note passage-work to avoid the use of the thumb and fifth finger on black keys; in the following examples the upper fingering is distinctly awkward, and the lower one much more comfortable and easy to control:

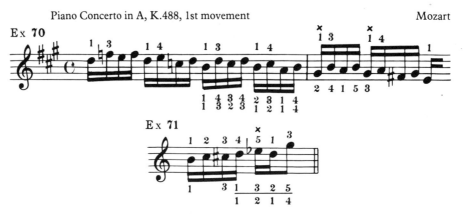

In examples **70** and **71** the fingerings *above* the notes are to be avoided.

Nevertheless there will be occasions when placing a thumb on a black key is not only unavoidable but also advantageous. It is obvious that the thumb will be used in all octaves and in all chords where the outer notes require the stretch of an octave; in addition, it can be used on black keys in the following cases:

(a)  Broken chord figures, such as one often meets in the piano writing of Beethoven; these, however, from the aspect of grouping, come within the category of ordinary chord-playing.

There are, incidentally, occasions when the rhythmic grouping of notes can influence fingering and the use of the thumb, as in Beethoven's Sonata, Op. 81a (third movement) where the upper fingering suggested is more likely to help the accentuation needed than the lower one. The basic chord position is, with the upper fingering, regarded as a second inversion, with the thumb extended to take the third as well as the fifth note of the chord.

(b) In exceptional cases the thumb may be taken on a black key at the top of a R.H. scale passage that finishes with an accent or sforzando.

Here the thumb can provide power that another finger (even when aided by arm-thrust or vigorous rotary action) would find hard to match. This applies also to the L.H., as shown by the suggested fingering, in Chopin's Third Scherzo, for bars 31 and 32 after the final 'Tempo I con fuoco'.

(c) In passages involving the playing of several black keys consecutively. In such cases it should be realized that to turn under the thumb on adjacent black keys to join two finger-groups is no more difficult than it is on adjacent white keys.

(d) In sequential passages it is sometimes better not to break an otherwise regular finger-pattern even if one statement of the sequence requires the use of a thumb on a black key. Brahms gives an excellent example of this in the first of his *51 Exercises* (which, when the L.H. is added, proves also to be a most useful 'cross-rhythm' study).

44

As mentioned above it is often a disadvantage to put a fifth finger on a black key (particularly if the R.H. is high in the treble or L.H. low in the bass). It is therefore sometimes better to change the order of playing the fingers in a rising passage in which the highest note is a black key. This also may avoid an extra turn-under of the thumb when the arms are extended towards the ends of the keyboard.

Concluding this topic, it may be remarked that in acquiring facility in putting the thumb on black keys it is excellent practice to play some of the scales that start on black keys with C major fingering.

## Fingering and articulation

The true art of fingering consists in finding, where possible, that fingering which enables the player to articulate (or punctuate) a passage in the way that is musically convincing (see the example from the Beethoven Sonata in E, Op. 109, third movement, first variation):

The fingering suggested may seem 'fussy' at first glance; it will be found that it compels the player to articulate the passage in the precise manner indicated by Beethoven in his manuscript. The conclusion to be drawn from this is that phrasing and fingering, should when possible go hand in hand. Before deciding on a fingering, ascertain if there is any call for a break in a phrase and, if there is, try to plan a fingering that will enable a change of hand position to commence after a break. This may not always be possible, but it would be manifestly absurd to spend time finding a legato fingering for a passage where a degree of punctuation is implicit in the phrase. The best fingering is that which is calculated to give the best effect from the aspects of tone, articulation and security; fingering 'for comfort' is only good if it helps security.

## Fingering to help accentuation

The mention of tone brings one to comment that in passages calling for brilliance and powerful tone it is often advisable to arrange the finger groups so that accents will be taken by strong fingers. (Accentuation in finger-work will also be helped by applying the 'undulating' principle as discussed in the previous chapter.) This may on occasion require an adjustment to be made to a recognized fingering pattern (such as a scale fingering) in order to suit the circumstances. Thus in the Third Piano Concerto of Beethoven there is in the first movement a fortissimo descending scale of C major with uneven rhythmic groupings which can be clearly and effectively shown with the following suggested fingering:

and in the Fourth Piano Concerto of Beethoven, first movement, it is advisable to adjust the L.H. chromatic scale fingering to assist accentuation of main beats.

## Fingering – long or short groups?

Fingering is a very personal matter influenced by variable things such as size of hand and the different views that may be taken of the style, tone and phrasing of the work under consideration. The basic principles of good fingering in thinking and playing in groups are however valid for all pianists; and one of the desirable aims should be to avoid unnecessary or restless changes of hand position. In this connection it is often useful to experiment, playing a passage with as few changes of position as may be possible, then to compare the effect obtained with a fingering which shifts position for each group of notes. The decision will be guided by the effect that is wanted: in a clearly defined and crisp rhythmic figure the choice will probably be to finger in separate short groups, whilst the same notes in a smoothly-flowing tranquil style will be more aptly played with as still a hand as possible:

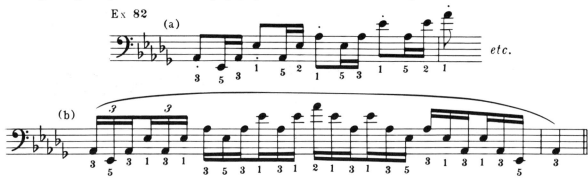

It becomes clear that the experienced player observes certain basic principles in the matter of fingering but that he will be constantly experimenting to find that which combines the required musical effect with the greatest degree of technical security. Knowing the 'rules' he will be prepared to break them if the result justifies the means.

It remains to mention briefly several random points relating to fingering:

(i) *Rearrangement of hands, etc.* It is a very prevalent habit to attempt to facilitate certain passages by playing them in ways which the composer did not intend, sometimes rearranging differently between the hands. The Beethoven Sonata in D minor, Op. 31 (first movement) suffers in this way in several editions.

Starting from bar 21 it is wrongly recommended that the R.H. should continue to play the eighth-note triplet figure whilst the L.H. crosses over to play the treble quarter-note melodic line. This ignores the fact that the bass-note D must be sustained for three bars; to hold this note with the pedal (necessary if played by R.H.) would blur the treble melody notes unpleasantly. Musically the rearrangement is also bad as the passage is thematically in the nature of a duo, with the bass strong and menacing, and the treble soft and pleading. In this case, each hand should have its own character and individuality. Beethoven's original distribution of this passage is right both for technical and dramatic reasons. In the bars (31 – 37) that follow, a further rearrangement of hands is sometimes suggested but this may throw the triplet eighth-notes 'out of phase'.

Such rearrangements abound and in general should be strongly discouraged. Exceptionally, minor rearrangements may be justified, perhaps in helping a small hand with an awkward stretch; but it should be a cardinal principle that notes should be played with the hand and in the manner that the composer intended. If, for reasons of the stretch, there is no alternative but to rearrange the passage, the player should conscientiously imagine what the effect would be if played as the composer intended and should aim to reproduce this exact effect. (Those addicted to altering and rearranging hands may be accused of practising 'Swindle-technique'!)

(ii) *Finger-substitution* It is seldom realized by the student how frequently it is necessary in legato-playing to substitute one finger for another on a note (to 'change fingers').

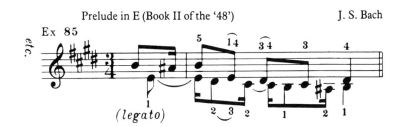

48

This is very often necessary in legato part-playing – it is a part of the standard equipment of organists. The technique of this needs thought and practice in order that the change may be made speedily and with no risk of the finger that 'takes over' re-sounding the note. A suggested exercise will be to play scales (slowly at first) changing fingers on every note:

The finger sounding the note will hold it down firmly until the other finger which takes over has settled itself in position. (Brahms gives a useful exercise to develop this facility in his *51 Exercises*.)

(iii) *Controlled sliding of fingers* There are many passages in which it is advantageous to be able to slide a finger in a controlled manner from a black key to the next white key. The 'knack' of controlling this sliding action has to be acquired, and here again Brahms gives a useful exercise, with variants. An example may be quoted from Beethoven's Sonata in C minor, Op. 111, where in the last pages of the *Arietta* the following passage occurs in the L.H., bar 134:

A large hand may be able to cope with the stretch of an octave, or more than an octave, (F natural to the F sharp above) played with the fifth and second fngers, but the majority of pianists will need to control the slide of the thumb to play this passage.

(iv) *Glissandos* Play all single-note glissandos on white keys with only the finger-nail making contact. The third (middle) finger is probably the best to use, as being well-balanced in the middle of the hand, and in forte passages it may be reinforced with the thumb at the back of the nail-joint. It is essential to keep the nail at right angles to the direction of movement or there may be some tearing of the flesh at the base of the nail. A descending glissando can often be played with the thumb-nail, but the thumb is not able to cover as wide a compass as the third finger.

In controlling glissandos: practise for a considerable time merely moving evenly over the surface of the keys, keeping a straight line, and being content to hear the regular 'click' of the nail moving across the keys. Apply pressure to produce sound only very gradually: glissandos supply an instance where pianissimo should precede forte-playing. Care needs to be taken with the final notes of glissandos (not to stop short nor to overshoot the mark) and it is generally better and neater to conclude with a fingered note, turning the hand to play with the finger that has executed the glissando, or with thumb.

If glissandos on the black keys are encountered, the technique is to play them with the backs of the three middle fingers; the friction caused in passing across the keys (particularly in negotiating the gaps between the groups of black keys) is shared between the three fingers and this should prevent any tearing of the skin. Do not attempt black key glissandos with the thumb or with only one finger!

For the playing of glissandos it is necessary to keep the wrist and fore-arm high, with the nail-phalanges of the fingers trailing. The attitude, especially with R.H. descending, is somewhat ungainly and awkward.

Double-note glissandos are occasionally encountered. It is essential to realize in such passages that if rising in the R.H. the nail-phalange of the upper finger of the two concerned must be 'trailing' (i.e. turned inward); if falling in the R.H. the thumb-nail must be trailing. In glissando sixths and octaves one of the fingers involved will be obliged to play with the flesh making contact. This can be painful, therefore allow most of the tone to be produced by the other finger playing on the finger-nail. Octave glissandos are, incidentally, impossible for the smallish hand owing to the necessity of holding a 'trailing' finger position.

(v) *Fallen finger-joints*  Many young players suffer from fallen finger-joints; normally it is the nail-joint which collapses inward creating a concave position. In playing, this cannot do otherwise than cause unevenness of tone as it would appear that the finger has lacked the strength to overcome key-resistance without collapsing, implying a wastage of the energy expended. To cure this completely may be a lengthy process, but is essential if tone-control is to be achieved. Exercises to cure this weakness will start with the fingers deliberately held out straight (on the knee, on a cushion or table-top), then proceed to press forward and downward, bending or flexing the fingers until they assume the desired rounded (convex) position. Ease the pressure if there is any sign of a finger collapsing. This kind of exercise may be applied to five-finger or other more extended positions on the keyboard, and it may be applied to single fingers and to any combination of fingers. If a young player is afflicted with 'fallen joints' when playing he should be warned not to hold a pen or pencil with a collapsed index or other finger when writing as this could aggravate the weakness.

(vi) *Safeguarding leaps to fifth finger*  One frequently meets leaps (in either hand) to fifth finger in which the interval involved is considerably greater than the stretch of the hand. The risk of inaccuracy is much reduced if the leap is in the first case practised as if it were to the octave and not to the single note concerned. Thus a dangerous leap of, say, an octave and a fifth, to be taken between thumb and fifth finger, is reduced to the smaller interval of a fifth (to be practised jumping with the thumbs);

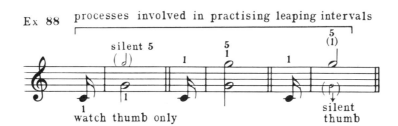

Ex 88  processes involved in practising leaping intervals

the player needs to know that he can accurately judge the imaginary distance of an octave-stretch, then to leap the required distance from thumb to thumb but slightly tilting the hand so that only the fifth finger sounds.

Piano Sonata in A minor, K.310, 3rd movement                    Mozart

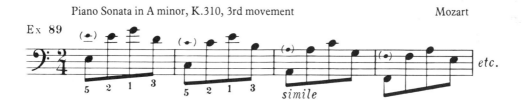

50

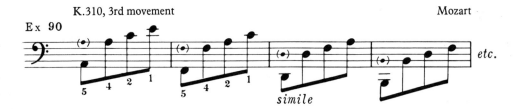

This method of reducing the risk in taking long intervals is useful applied to the left hand in valse-like basses:

(vi) *The approach to dotted-note rhythms*   The technique for such figures as are found in the Second Impromptu of Chopin and in the G minor Rhapsody of Brahms needs a clear understanding if consistent accuracy is to be achieved:

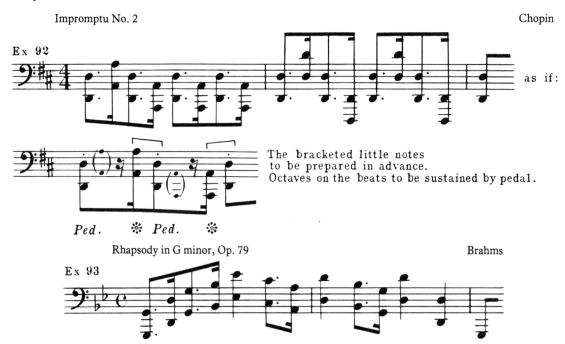

The use of the sustaining pedal is assumed in order to sustain the dotted eighth-notes for their full value; having then played the first octave, the following sixteenth-note will be prepared in advance. With the fingers safely covering the sixteenth-note, the player's eyes move to guide the quick accurate aim of the hand to the next dotted eighth-note. The process is then repeated through the passage. (Every short note is prepared in advance by 'feeling' for the required keys; from the prepared position, after sounding the short note the hand makes an unprepared leap, guided by the eyes to each dotted eighth-note.) Any other process than the above is likely to lead to a lengthening of the sixteenth-notes and a lack of rhythmic precision. Playing from memory is presumed in all such cases; it is important that the other hand should be trained to play by 'feel' of the notes and without any visual glance whatever. One must not be tempted to look for one moment away from the hand which is making the quick leap.

(viii) *The playing of sustained repeated notes or chords*   It is often found that sustained notes and chords are played too abruptly. Schumann, in his G minor Sonata, Op. 22, second movement, writes *Getragen* for the repeated chords in the L.H., implying that the sound must be carried over from one repetition to the next without any break of sound.

Schubert clearly expects the same effect in the *Andante* of his A major Sonata, Op. 120. This kind of repetition is played with the wrist lifting but allowing the fingers to cling to the notes until the last possible moment before re-sounding. If the touch of the piano is well adjusted it will be found possible to sound the notes of a repeated chord again before the keys have risen fully to the top; this implies that the dampers in turn will not have effected a silencing of the previous chord before the next one is played. There is therefore a continuous unbroken sound. To produce this effect it is necessary to have a sensitive feeling for the keys and a supple freedom of the wrist; to play from the fore-arm with a stiff and unmoving wrist will cause the fingers to lift to the surface of the key, and the dampers will be effective in breaking off any sound.

(ix) *The crossing of hands*   When any crossing of hands is necessary it must be decided whether to cross over or under. Usually it is better for the hand which makes the move to pass over the hand which remains in the normal position. There will however be occasions when, perhaps to avoid the risk of dropping too heavily on a key, it may be wiser for the hand which crosses to pass under; an example of this is found in Beethoven's *Das Lebewohl* Sonata, Op. 81a, in bar 65 towards the end of the exposition of the first movement when the L.H. crosses to take a quick up-beat minor third in the treble clef. This minor third is immediately repeated on the following main beat, and it is advisable for the L.H. in this case to pass under the R.H. (which is holding a B flat in the bass clef) in order to reduce the possibility of undesirable accentuation of the up-beat eighth-notes.

If a cross-over covers a large amount of the keyboard with L.H. reaching high in the treble or R.H. far down in the bass it is generally better not to use the thumb when playing in such an extreme position (though this may be unavoidable if the hand which crosses is required to play a chord); to play the thumb in such circumstances causes a stretching-across of greater distance and is therefore less comfortable than would be the case using, say, an extended index finger.

52

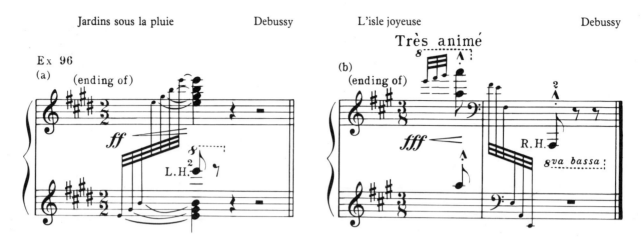

Ex 96
(a) (ending of)

(b) (ending of)
Très animé

Occasionally the hands are required to play in partially crossed or interlocked positon. In such cases there can be a danger of fingers colliding, and to avoid this the hand playing on any black keys (which though shorter are of course slightly raised) will normally take the upper position. This is very clearly demonstrated in Villa-Lobos's *O Polichinello*. In cases where both hands contain some black keys, as in the middle section of the first movement of Bartók's Suite, Op. 14, it may be necessary to experiment to find the most practicable solution of the difficulty.

O Polichinello          Villa-Lobos

Ex 97
(a) Vivo

*Col Ped. sempre*

Suite, Op. 14, No. 1          Bartók

(b) Allegretto

*cresc. poco a poco*

L.H. over; L.H. thumb between R.H. 1 and 2

CHAPTER IV

# The art of shaping a phrase

When we come to consider what is involved in shaping a musical phrase it becomes apparent at once that this is a complex matter. A number of factors contribute to the final effect, and it is important that we should recognize and be able to make use of these different elements in combining them intelligently. Analysis, which is a mental activity of taking something to pieces, comes first; art, in this case, lies in a putting-together again to make a continuous whole. As no two personalities are identical, no two artists are likely to put the various elements together in precisely the same way or in the same proportions, even though both may start with the same basic material and with similar training and outlook. Thus it is that we come to have different interpretations from equally intelligent and gifted performers – and this can apply to the views taken of individual phrases as it can also to the conceptions of whole works. Each will see the composer's intentions through the medium of his own personality.

It can be acknowledged that intuition plays a large part in many fine performances, but this intuition must be based upon solid, well-founded musicianship. It is necessary to have some knowledge of the styles and customs of different musical periods, and to know something of the characteristics of the composer with whose work we are concerned; and if there is any factual information available about the particular work which we are studying this also should be taken into account before we allow ourselves the luxury of letting our imagination run riot with 'hunches' about interpretation. Furthermore, any intuitive hunch must be open to justification by analysis and reasoning. We need, therefore, to have what may be called an 'informed imagination'.

From the technical aspect, the fundamentals, or what one might call the raw materials of musicianly phrasing, are: (i) rhythm; (ii) punctuation; and (iii) the use of tone in moulding a phrase.

## (i) Rhythm

To consider some aspects of rhythm first: rhythm in music should be felt as a physical sensation. It is not enough merely to think of rhythm as 'counting time' according to the number of beats there may be in a bar or measure, necessary though that may be. Rhythm and movement are indivisibly associated. It is probably true to say that in all parts of the world rhythm was the first manifestation of the musical instinct – rhythm associated, as an expression of emotion, with bodily movement to the clapping of hands or the beating of drums; it is the basic element in music. The earliest instruments would almost certainly be percussive instruments, and in this connection it is significant that some of the more primitive tribes of Central Africa today use complex rhythmic drum patterns that can baffle a European ear and mind. But we need go no further than the Balkans to appreciate the fascinating diversity of irregular rhythms in folk-music.

Musical sounds which are not held together by some kind of rhythmic organization are chaotic and meaningless, and it is clear that rhythm not only brings coherence to music but provides the pulse that gives it life. Music, in its special nature of 'revealing' as it unfolds, inevitably involves a progress through time, and the creative use of time is as essential to music as the creative use of space is to painting. In the performance of music we recognize that whether a tempo is fast or slow there is of necessity a sense of progress, and the very concept of rhythm implies that this must be an organized movement towards a cadence or climax point – and this will be closely associated with tonal gradation. We cannot know what the dynamics of a work should be unless (and until) we have grasped its rhythmic shape. In the journey through time, rhythm in its widest sense embraces a consideration of everything from (a) the relationships of time-values within a bar, to (b) bar-rhythms, (c) phrase-lengths and (d) to the grasp of the formal designs of complete musical structures, the sections of which must balance. One is tempted to go further in reflecting that rhythm is fundamental to life and existence: there is the movement of the earth round the sun giving the rhythm of the seasons; there is the movement of the moon around the earth producing the rhythm of the tides; and there is the movement of the earth revolving on its axis to produce the rhythm of night and day – one could continue ad infinitum.

For the player the learning of rhythmic patterns in a phrase demands (i) the establishing of a firm basic pulse (never start playing until you have decided on a tempo); (ii) that the player should think (and play) through to the next beat or bar; in a continuous phrase one must invariably think from bar to bar with never a comma or delay on the bar-line; (iii) that in the learning process it is helpful to tap (or sing) the rhythmic pattern involved away from the keyboard; the difficulty of finding unfamiliar notes on the keyboard may cause hesitation and prevent the precision of rhythm that is sought – and trying to master difficulties of notes and of rhythm simultaneously may cause physical tension.

Here are a few examples of rhythms which could be tapped out at both slow and fast tempi; the resourceful player or teacher will be able to supply many more from actual works. To count aloud the basic pulse whilst tapping will also be helpful:

A variant in acquiring rhythmic independence and control is to beat time as a conductor whilst humming various patterns. When transferring tapped or hummed rhythms to the keyboard it is of course vital to time the production of tone with the utmost precision.

In the case of syncopated notes remember that syncopation is an abnormality of rhythm and, as with other abnormalities, it should be measured against what is normal; hence it is necessary to provide a firm main beat against which the syncopation is precisely timed:

Piano Sonata in C minor, K.457, 3rd movement                                    Mozart

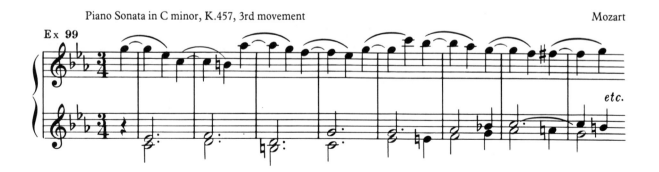

An understanding and a grasp of 'cross-rhythms' is necessary. The student should master 'threes against twos' whilst in a relatively early stage of learning; in this easiest of cross-rhythms simple arithmetic explains the working and the timing of the two independent rhythmic patterns as follows:

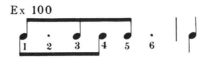

and it should be clear that if these patterns are tapped together, the rhythm which will be heard is:

When counted aloud this becomes: 'One, two and three'. In the learning stages attention should primarily be given to tapping the triplet group with precision; the second unit of the couplet will fit evenly and exactly between the second and third units of the triplet.

When one progresses to 'threes against fours' and other more complicated combinations, the 'breakdown' into simple arithmetic ceases to be practicable. Instead, one needs first to acquire fluency and control by tapping and playing each individual pattern; in putting them together one should aim primarily to fit the main beats with precision; it is then helpful to concentrate (with both hands playing) the attention − and to give more tone − to one hand at a time, as in the following kind of exercise:

The obvious aim is to train oneself to hear and to listen to two rhythms independently, and to be able to tap and to play with complete control.

Extending this survey to bar-rhythms: most phrases will be found to consist of two, four and eight-bar lengths, though multiples of threes are not uncommon, and one should be alert in looking for changing patterns and for occasional extensions of normal-length phrases. With the normal four-bar phrases we often find an alternation of 'strong-bar, weak-bar'; nevertheless there are many works written in which the weak bar commences the phrase, and it is essential to get this rhythmic scanning correct if we are to capture the accentuation and the musical meaning as the composer intended. In a number of Beethoven's scherzo movements in $\frac{3}{4}$ time we find that the first bar is in fact a 'weak' bar; and when we adjust ourselves to this 'weak-strong' alternation he is liable to catch us on the wrong foot in his Trio sections by reversing the accentuation to 'strong-weak'. A good example of this is found in the *Moonlight* Sonata, Op. 27, No.2, where Beethoven commences his Scherzo as follows:

Ex 103

This is much as if he had commenced the movement on the third beat of a $^6_4$ bar. In the Trio of this movement Beethoven reverses the bar-rhythm and starts on the strong bar (after a syncopated quarter-note up-beat).

Ex 104

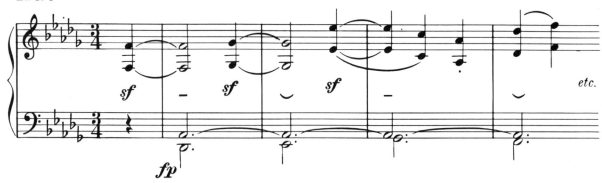

Other similar instances are to be found; in addition, there are occasional ambiguous movements such as the Scherzo of Op. 110, where it appears that Beethoven changes his stress after the first eight bars. (See Chapter V for comments on Op. 110.) In the Trio of this movement he writes eight-bar phrases which are interrupted by a three-bar phrase. We find also a series of three-bar phrases in the first movement of the Sonata in E flat, Op, 81a (*Das Lebewohl*) occurring in bars 95 – 109:

Ex 105

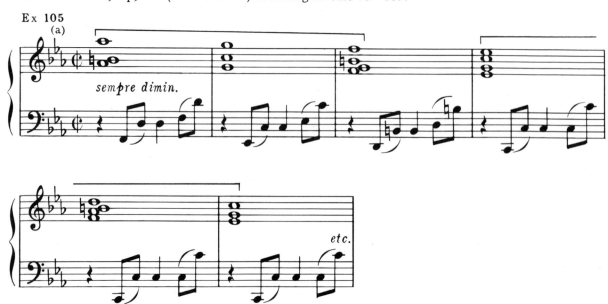

These are founded on the opening notes of the movement:

Three-bar phrases must be recognized when 'scanning' a work.

It should be noted that it is generally in quick movements that it is important to get the relative stresses of the bars in the right relationship; this matter is less obvious in slow movements. As Donald Tovey once said facetiously: 'It is easy to hear the relationship of a crochet to two quavers, but who among us would recognize precisely the same relationship in a period of one hour followed by two half-hours.' A well-known case of changing bar-rhythms is found in the Finale of Haydn's *English* Sonata in C, Hob. 50: in this case Haydn starts the movement, which is in quick triple time, with an up-beat to a 'weak' bar (precisely as Beethoven does with the Scherzo of the *Moonlight*), but Haydn then proceeds to a three-bar period followed by one of two bars, and throughout the movement there are unexpected changes back and forth from three bars to two bars. As these changes of step are often associated with quite outrageous harmonic twists (Haydn finishes one innocent C major phrase with a B major chord and a C minor phrase finishes with a D flat chord) it becomes obvious that Haydn, who was something of a wit, is here indulging his sense of humour. To do justice to this brilliant movement the player must 'scan' these irregular bar-rhythms carefully or the stresses are likely to be misplaced.

Ex 106

Interesting examples of irregular lengths of phrases are found in the first movement of Mozart's Sonata in D, K576, near the end of the exposition (bars 46–53) and in the development section.

Before leaving the subject of bar-rhythms it may be of interest to compare the styles of notation (in time-values) which different composers use to convey very similar tempi: thus Beethoven in the *Appassionata* Sonata writes his second main theme as follows:

Ex 107  **Allegro assai**

Chopin writes his Fourth Scherzo in the following very different manner:

Ex 108  **Presto**

but the speed of Chopin's dotted half-note is practically identical with the speed of Beethoven's dotted quarter-note. We feel Chopin's rhythm to be a one-in-a-bar movement and that he is presenting us with a four-bar phrase; one bar of Beethoven's quadruple time would cover the whole of Chopin's subject (as far as the fifth bar) but in itself is only the first bar of a more extended theme. Beethoven's movement is marked *Allegro assai*, that of Chopin – *Presto*.

With the mention of relative speeds we come to the next problem: that of feeling and deciding on the pace which will best realize the character of the theme, phrase or movement which is under consideration. When we talk of tempo it is necessary to determine what we mean by the 'right' tempo. It should aim to be the speed which the composer had in mind when writing; and this implies that it is that pace which permits the musical meaning and the emotional significance of the work to show to the best effect. It must be a speed which will present the rhythmic flow in such a way that the structure and proportions of a work are clear, and it must allow for technical precision and clear articulation.

How then can we arrive at a performing tempo which fulfils the above conditions? The first and most important factor in deciding on a suitable tempo will be the composer's time-signature, which will tell us in what pulse or 'unit of time' he is thinking. For example, if we are intended to feel four quarter-note beats in a bar his time-signature will be $\frac{4}{4}$ or the sign C for common-time; he may however write ₵, signifying *alla breve* which in turn tells us that he is thinking of two half-note beats per bar. This will generally suggest a faster tempo, though there are cases such as the second movement of Beethoven's First Piano Concerto, in which a genuinely slow tempo still carries the *alla breve* sign ₵; the character of the theme here suggests that Beethoven wishes the performer to avoid the slightest stress on the second and fourth crotchets.

Ex 109  Largo

*etc.*

(very slow two in a bar with, normally, no tonal stress on second and fourth quarter-note beats)

Certainly it must be emphasized that any Italian tempo marking such as *Adagio* or *Allegro* carries a direct reference to the unit of time, i.e. quarter-note in the case of $\frac{4}{4}$ time and half-note in the case of *alla breve* (or $\frac{2}{2}$). It should incidentally be borne in mind that we may well find some pieces which are basically slow in tempo but which carry many quick notes; Ravel's beautiful piece *Ondine* is one such case with a slowly unfolding melody line accompanied almost throughout by an atmospheric background of rapid thirty-second-notes.

Ex 110  Lent

*etc.*

*très doux et très expressif*

In the case of the triple time-signatures we must judge from the general character which unit of time is intended; with the Chopin Scherzos (including the Fourth quoted above), the marking of *Presto*, taken in conjunction with the fact that the fastest time-values used are eighth-notes, establishes without doubt that the $\frac{3}{4}$ time-signature is to be felt as a brisk one-in-a-bar.

Scherzo No. 2 in B flat minor                    Chopin

Ex 111

Presto

*etc.*

(One in a bar = four-bar phrases)

A $\frac{3}{4}$ movement using thirty-second-notes (or sixty-fourth-notes) will just as clearly be established at once as a true three-in-a-bar, even without such a marking as *Adagio*; an example of this would be the *Sarabande* of Bach's B flat Partita (which carries no tempo marking).

Ex 112

*etc.*

With compound duple time such as $\frac{6}{8}$ or $\frac{6}{4}$ the operative word is 'duple', and such rhythms will normally be felt as two-in-a-bar and not six, though here also some $\frac{6}{8}$ movements such as Chopin's Berceuse (and his Nocturne in D flat) are slow-moving and highly decorated.

Berceuse, Op. 57

Chopin

Quicker examples of $\frac{6}{8}$ will not contain time-values shorter than sixteenth-notes and will be mostly written in eighth-notes as in Beethoven's Finale to the Sonata in E flat, Op. 31.

The same reasoning applies to the other compound time-signatures, $\frac{9}{8}$ and $\frac{12}{8}$, which will be felt as three-in-a-bar and four-in-a-bar respectively; the unit of time in these cases being the dotted quarter-note. A good example of compound quadruple time is found in Chopin's Barcarolle.

In this important matter of finding the correct unit of time it may help to quote a few more examples: in Mozart we find a firm, steady march-like four-in-a-bar in the opening of the A minor Sonata, K.310.

Ex 116

The *Adagio* of the C minor Sonata, K.457 is also a true four-in-a-bar of a different tempo and character.

Ex 117

The faster four-in-a-bar movements must not become *alla breve*, and the slower movements should not drag to a laboured eight-in-a-bar. Several of Mozart's Rondo Finales are *alla breve*, needing to flow along with two main pulses per bar; examples include the two Sonatas in B flat, K.281 and K.333.

K.281 (Rondeau)

Ex 118

It is interesting to note, incidentally, that a number of the Finales to his piano sonatas have strong hints of concerto treatment in the shape of a quiet (solo) statement of a theme followed by a strong (tutti) re-statement of the same theme. A good example is found in K.333,

Ex 119

and it is clear that there is the same intention in the third movement of the Sonata in C, K.330.

With the triple rhythms we find that the typical Minuets of Bach, Haydn and Mozart have three steady beats per bar,

Piano Sonata in A, Hob. 26, Minuet al Rovescio                                    Haydn

This Minuet and the Trio which follows are also to be read backwards (bar by bar)

Piano Sonata, K282                                                                Mozart

whilst in Beethoven we find many Scherzos that are three-in-a-bar with contrasting Trios to follow that are one-in-a-bar; for example the Scherzo of Beethoven's Sonata in C, Op.2, No.3, has a first section that is a true three-in-a-bar and a Trio (at the same tempo) that must certainly be felt as one-in-a-bar.

It is important to recognize that many works change the 'unit of time' within a movement without altering either the number of beats in a bar or the metronomic speed. A good example is found in the opening movement of Beethoven's Sonata in C, Op.2, No.3, which begins with four quick (and strict) beats per bar,

Ex 123

but from bar 27 (G minor) there is a clear change to two half-note beats per bar.

Ex 124

This permits a degree of flexibility in the playing of the melodic eighth-notes; however, at bar 39 there is a return to the strict four quarter-notes, (these run on until bar 45);

Ex 125

here there is a brief linking passage (with turns) which is felt as two per bar, and from bars 47–61 a new theme is introduced; this must be regarded as one-in-a-bar if the arch of the phrases is to be shaped without any disturbing stress on the third beats of the bars.

Ex 126

From bar 61 to the end of the exposition (bar 90) the original four-per-bar rules supreme. Such changes as are described are a legitimate part of the technique of composition, giving rhythmic variety within a longish movement without interfering with the steady onward 'march' and the unity of the structure. Another of the many examples from Beethoven is found in the first movement of the *Waldstein* Sonata, Op.53, where the opening is in a straightforward four quarter-notes per bar

Ex 127
Allegro con brio

and the second subject (bar 35, E major) changes to one-in-a-bar without any tempo change.

Ex 128

Here Beethoven, in the manuscript marks a long slur covering four bars; this, combined with the one-in-a-bar feeling, indicates to the performer that a long smooth phrase is wanted, unbroken by accents.

A recognition of the appropriate unit of time will prevent a complete misjudgment of tempo but may not necessarily give the precision with regard to pace that we are seeking. The usual Italian markings give an indication, but they are at best generalizations (and remember that Bach seldom gives even these indications). Metronome markings, even when they are the composer's own, are not always to be trusted – one hears of cases of eminent composers jotting down metronome marks whilst humming over themes away from an instrument, only to admit when it comes to performance, that their metronome suggestions have been faulty (generally too fast); there is also the possibility of a metronome which, with badly-adjusted mechanism, ticks away faster or slower than it should. In the choice of tempo it can safely be asserted that the speed should not be so fast that the quickest passages cannot be played clearly and coherently without apparent hurry; but that criterion does not extend to the consideration of slow tempi. For assessment of a slow tempo let the pianist imagine that if he were a conductor he could still keep his baton moving at the rate of the slowest pulse without breaking into half-beats. An example would be the opening *Grave* of Beethoven's Sonata in C minor, Op.13 (*Pathétique*); this is an extremely slow four-in-a-bar which must never be allowed to degenerate into eight-in-a-bar; this incidentally is not to deny that the student in learning the movement may find it advisable to subdivide some beats and some bars in order to get the detailed time-values correct.

Ex 129

We find in this matter of tempo, which is a problem that is always with us throughout our experience as musicians, that the ideal tempo for a work often cannot be crystallized from its first subject alone, and that it is in fact invariably wise to consider the characters and demands of all the thematic material and all sections of a work before coming to a final decision as to what is indeed the best tempo for the opening

66

and for the whole movement. Instances that come to mind are the first movement of Beethoven's Fourth Piano Concerto and the first movement of the *Appassionata* Sonata. The opening of the Fourth Concerto is so beautiful that most pianists will be tempted to linger over it, only to find that lingering has induced a slower tempo than can be tolerated for the other material of the movement; there will be disturbing changes of tempo unless the player has found a common denominator of pace that will suit all sections of the work. The *Appassionata* also often suffers very considerable changes of tempo even in the first two pages – possibly a too slow start, followed by a much-quickened section with repeated notes; a broadening of the 'big tune', then 'fast and furious' for the sixteenth-notes in both hands. Such misplaced changes of pace inevitably ruin the structural growth of a symphonic movement. There should be a constant checking of one section against another to ensure uniformity of tempo within a movement.

Consideration of the various factors involved in the above comments on tempo brings one to the conclusion that a feeling for the right kind of pulse or unit of time is more important than mere metronomic speed, and that within certain relatively restricted margins two different personalities can take different tempi for the same work, and each can be equally convincing in his own way. Let it therefore be admitted that there is no such thing as an 'absolute' tempo which alone is right and all others therefore wrong. We have only to recall the frequent fast tempi of Toscanini which could be so brilliant – until one heard the slower tempi of Klemperer which penetrated so deeply into the inner heart of the music and yet which never lost the steady pulse of life moving relentlessly forward throughout the whole work.

*Rubato* No discussion of rhythmic problems is complete without a reference to rubato – literally 'robbed time', meaning: to give slightly extra time to some notes of a phrase at the expense of others which will be equally slightly shortened, so that the give-and-take of time balances.

Rubato is, in many kinds of music, an essential contributing factor aiming to give greater freedom of expression. It is a means of emphasis that may, or may not, be associated with additional tonal stress. There are occasions when the character of the music demands the tonal restraint of 'sempre piano' or 'sempre pianissimo' in order not to break an atmosphere; in such cases the only available means of emphasis is then to give a little extra time to a note, or to a segment of a phrase, enabling it to assert its significance. But when it is necessary to give considerable power and breadth to the climax of a section (or of a work) it may certainly be appropriate to make a crescendo and a broadening of time simultaneously; the tempo will normally be resumed by making a discreet accelerando leading back to the original pulse.

There are however instances in rubato when the element of accelerando may come first in building-up excitement or agitation in a work; the slackening or relaxing of the tempo would then come when the crisis is past. In all cases subtlety and judgment are required in taking up the tempo naturally and convincingly without giving a disturbing 'jolt' to the basic pulse, and it is important to realize precisely when the normal flow of tempo should be resumed after completing a passage that has required the flexibility of 'rubato'.

Rubato is particularly associated with the music of romantic composers and, especially for pianists, with the works of Chopin. Flexibility in phrasing that approximates to 'rubato' is however fully justified in shaping the more florid melodic lines of Bach. A rigidly mechanical playing of the beautiful melodic line in Bach's F sharp minor Prelude (Book II of the '48') would be unthinkable, but flexibility in dealing with decorative melodic lines of the Baroque era should not extend to breaking the regularity of an underlying rhythmic pulse: the expressive freedom will remain within the beat.

Ex 130

The same understanding of rubato will apply to Mozart who in his piano sonatas and concertos often borrows from his operatic experience and writes melodies for piano that call for a *bel canto* style. These will be treated with a certain vocal freedom but, again, without interfering with the steady forward progress of the basic rhythm. In the example quoted, the bars (Nos. 2 and 4) with eighth-notes may be played with discreet flexibility.

Piano Concerto in A, K.488                                                                            Mozart

Ex 131          Allegro

It may be said therefore that in the earlier music, the flexibility that is tasteful and appropriate will be a 'short-term' rubato, within the underlying pulse of the music.

Following Mozart, Beethoven was a composer whose style was continually evolving and developing, and in the matter of rubato a very different approach is needed for his earlier works as compared with what may be right for his 'middle' period, and for his late works. As stated earlier in this chapter, the melodic line starting at bar 27, in the first movement of the C major Sonata, Op. 2, will require a degree of flexibility within an *alla breve* beat as a contrast to the strictness of the previous four-in-a-bar of that movement. Similar examples will be found elsewhere in Beethoven's earlier works, and they conform, in this matter of 'flexibility within the pulse', to the practice of Mozart and Haydn. In Beethoven's middle period we find in such works as the *Waldstein* (Op. 53) and *Appassionata* (Op. 57) Sonatas that his enormous rhythmic 'drive', combined with his feeling for structural growth, will not permit 'liberties' to be taken, other than the 'built-in' ritardandos which he marks. Even so, one must avoid mechanical strictness, particularly at peak points in the slow movements.

When one turns to Op. 81a (*Das Lebewohl*) it seems that more freedom is called for in giving expression to the intense personal feeling of the second movement. Later, in the *Adagio* of the *Hammerklavier* Sonata, Op. 106, third movement, the performer's continual problem is to combine the utmost freedom of expression for the sections commencing bars 27 and 113 (anticipating the style and freedom that are normally thought desirable for Chopin's works) with the slow but steady and relentless rhythmic progress necessary for the unfolding of the mighty structure of this movement.

68

Ex 132

Finally, with Beethoven, one comes to the last Sonatas where, for instance, we find in Op. 110, which is examined in more detail in the following chapter on 'Analysis and Imagination', that in bars 5 and 6 leading to the *Arioso* he marks the freedoms of time and tone that he feels to be necessary with fifteen directions in the space of two bars. (Is there any other music where such detailed instructions for performance are given as in these last Sonatas?)

One also asks the question: does the first movement of Op. 111, in a large section of the recapitulation, not enlarge the normal scope of rubato? Here Beethoven presents us with subtle freedoms of tempo within a movement which has tremendous driving energy. Between bars 116 and 132 he gives clear instructions for a large-scale rubato: for two bars we have a theme stated at full tempo, but at bar 118 there is a *meno allegro* for the first part of a decorated statement of the same theme, which then continues with a *ritardando* into a short *adagio*. In bar 122 the original tempo is resumed, and in bar 124 the same theme is stated (at full tempo) in the sub-dominant key again to be followed after two bars by *meno allegro* and *ritardando*; but in bar 128 a four-bar section of increasing speed (*poi a poi sempre più Allegro*) begins and leads to a lasting return of *Tempo I* (from bar 132).

The freedoms of time throughout this section are a part of the architecture of the movement. The player will need to spend much thought and to use sound judgment in presenting it logically and convincingly; if this can be imaginatively and successfully accomplished the final return to *Tempo I* can be the most gripping passage of the entire movement.

Rubato in the playing of Chopin's works is often greatly exaggerated. His contemporaries stated of his playing that frequently he did not keep his hands together, and it is believed that he was in the habit of keeping a strict rhythm with the L.H. whilst allowing expressive freedom to the R.H. in shaping melodic decorations. Here are typical cases where such treatment may well apply:

Nocturne, Op. 9, No. 1                                                                                                    Chopin

Impromptu No. 2                                                          Chopin

Ex 134

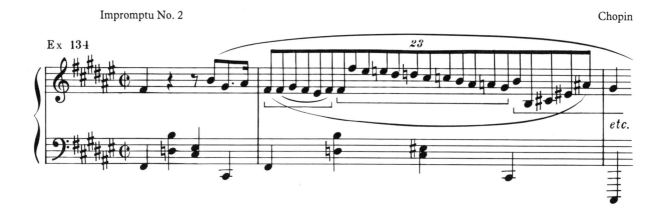

Ballade No. 4, in F minor, Op. 52                                        Chopin

Ex 135

The ornamentation is entirely individual and the most brilliant arabesques are always melodic and graceful. Such passages in Chopin's works are generally not rhythmically grouped by him though in some editions they are to be found subdivided in somewhat questionable manner; almost invariably they should be regarded according to the individual melodic shapes of which they are constructed. Thus in the example from the Nocturne the first eleven notes will be subdivided in one's mind as 3 + 5 + 3, the middle group being a written-out 'turn'; the following bar of 22 notes in the R.H. suggests the sub-divisions of 4 + 10 + 5 + 3: first an incomplete turn (a middle F omitted), followed by a descending chromatic scale over which the staccato dots indicate rubato in lingering at the top then increasing speed in falling to the note C on which there is a five-note 'turn'. The whole decoration is rounded-off by a triplet falling from the dominant F. The ideal performance is for the R.H. to be played independently as a series of free melodic patterns against an unyielding rhythm in the L.H. Most emphatically, what must not be done is to divide the decorative notes by the number of beats in the bar (6 into 22 etc. . . !), nor to play the passage mechanically and rigidly. It is only necessary in this case for the first note of the passage and the first note of the next bar to fit precisely with the left hand.

The other examples should be regarded similarly, and suggestions for grouping are given.

To keep the L.H. moving steadily whilst permitting R.H. flexibility would seem to be a logical development of the kind of freedom that is justifiable in the playing of Baroque and early classical music, on both of which styles Chopin was largely brought up. Chopin however often extends the period of rubato beyond the 'flexibility-within-the-pulse' of the earlier composers.

The convincing use of rubato demands that the player must have a well-developed sense of a strong basic pulse to which he can return without wavering; when abused, the introduction of rubato can lead to rhythmic distortion and a weakening (or breaking up) of a musical structure − also to sentimentality. The truly musical rubato leaves the listener unaware of its use.

It is no paradox to say that rubato should only be permitted to those who can play in time!

## (ii) Punctuation

Punctuation, which is another of the 'raw materials' of phrasing, would be a relatively straightforward matter if we were concerned only to find the cadence points. The scope of punctuation in phrasing must however be extended to cover what is more correctly termed 'articulation'. A phrase is a complete musical sentence of several bars length; articulation deals with the slurred or detached treatment of notes or groups of notes within a phrase, such as the following simple figure:

Ex 136

this has the first note connected to the second by a legato slur, whilst the third and fourth notes are given staccato dots; it is a common fault of students to slur the second note to the third. It should not be necessary to point out that there is no slur connecting the second note to the third, therefore only the first note is slurred to the second and the last three notes are all detached. Articulation is thus concerned with the various possible subdivisions of a phrase, and the obvious simile is with the words and syllables that constitute a sentence in a language. In a language that we know, we are aware that each syllable and each word plays its part in contributing to the meaning of the whole sentence; similarly each subdivision of a musical phrase has its part to play in giving character to the whole phrase.

To present a musical phrase intelligently it must first be analysed and split into its component parts just as one should recognize the individual words in a spoken sentence*. The greater art then lies in

---

*Amusicalphraseplayedwithoutscanningmaywellbesomewhatlikethissentence.
Though continuity of delivery is needed the player must realize where are the subdivisions, as with the above words.

72

putting the subdivisions together again to make a well-shaped and rhythmically-flowing complete phrase; if, in performance, we are made too aware of the subdivisions the phrase will lose its rhythmic flow and coherency, and will sound disjointed. Though we need in the early stages of learning a work to make sure that we are 'scanning' the phrases as the composer intended, the final result must sound spontaneous and never sectionally analytical.

Sinfonia from Partita No. 2 in C minor                                                                                       J. S. Bach

Ex 137  Andante

In this example it is desirable to maintain an unbroken legato in the R.H. but following the first half-bar (ending on C) the second half of the bar suggests a qualifying phrase in parenthesis, after which (second bar, second note) the main discourse is resumed. Subtle tonal differences can convey the implied articulation without breaking either the legato or the rhythm.

The interpretation of the works of the earlier composers presents special difficulties, as it is only rarely that we find any marks of articulation such as slurs and dots; and it may be helpful to give some examples from the works of J.S. Bach. (All Bach quotations are from the untouched Henle Urtext; many editions of Bach are badly over-edited.) In the absence of so-called 'marks of expression' we look, among other things, for recurring patterns of notes:

Italian Concerto, 1st movement

Ex 138

Prelude in A flat (Book II of the '48')

Ex 139

for the contours of rising or falling sequences:

Prelude in E (Book II of the '48')

Ex 140

Italian Concerto, 3rd movement

Ex 141

for changes of pitch (as with a string player bowing on another string):

Prelude in F sharp minor (Book II of the '48')

Ex 142

this clearly suggests:

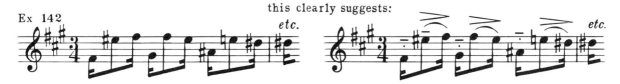

With Bach, clear examples of the beginning and end of subdivisions of phrases can be found in movements from his Suites in which several of the old dance-forms which he uses have their recognized conventions of starting on particular beats of the bar; thus the tradition is that gavottes will start on the third quarter-note of four beats in the bar (often, but not invariably, written as an *alla breve*), and that bourrées will start on the fourth quarter-note up-beat of a brisk *alla breve* tempo. Throughout these dance-movements all phrases and subdivisions will start on the same beat of the bar. The *Allemande* of the C minor Partita offers a good example of recurring patterns: in this case groups of eight sixteenth-notes start on the second note of a group of four, and two separate melodic shapes share this rhythmic grouping. In a gentle *alla breve* tempo these three up-beat sixteenth-notes commence consistently before the main first and third quarter-notes of the bars, as follows:

Ex 143

Examples such as the above are not difficult to analyse; in performing them the player should be aware of the subdivisions without breaking the continuity of movement. There is no uniformity of treatment for such cases; frequently the groups will be so closely linked that no audible subdivision is heard (as in the words of a sentence spoken all in one breath). In other instances a minimal break in tone by shortening the duration (but not the actual time-value of a note) may add crispness and clarity to the phrasing; examples of this occur in the two *Bourrées* of the English Suite in A minor where, in the second full bar of each *Bourrée* (and frequently later) there will be a slightly staccato shortening of the third-beat quarter-notes in order to make clear the subdivision of the groups (the rhythm in these cases remains quite strict).

Ex 144 BOURRÉE I

Ex 145 BOURRÉE II

Even when he is not writing in the dance-forms Bach habitually gives a unity to his themes and phrases by starting them on the same part of a bar and on occasion he may use and combine two patterns.

English Suite in A minor

Ex 146 PRELUDE
1st Theme

Ex 147 2nd theme

This uniformity in starting contrasting subjects of a movement on the same part of a bar is of course not confined to Bach.

The mention above of the shortening of a note by staccato playing makes it necessary to define the difference between the rhythmic time-value of a note and the actual duration of sound that is heard before the note is damped. Only in legato playing are notes held audibly for their full value; staccato playing automatically deprives a note of a fraction of its audible sound though rhythm is in no way affected, and a following note or chord must be sounded at its own precise moment in time. The difference between the true time-value of a note and the actual duration which such a note is permitted to sound before damping is fundamental to the articulation of a phrase, and it is vital that no misunderstanding should exist on so basic a point.

Acceptance of the truth that there is a difference between a written time-value and the audible duration of a note ostensibly possessing the same time-value, prompts the thought that in contrapuntal playing we have at times to deal with two-part writing where both parts are to be played by the same hand. In such cases it frequently happens that one part will require a smooth legato whilst the other part may need to be detached; the detached notes must not be allowed to interfere with the smooth delivery of the other voice or part. Many examples of this are found in the part-writing of Bach; here is one from the B flat Fugue of the first Book of the '48':

Here the upper part will be played with an even legato whilst the lower part of eighth-notes will be played staccato, losing approximately half of their full time-value. The passage should sound in the following manner:

but it is often heard wrongly with the repeated notes of the lower part causing a lift of the upper part to give an effect of couplets instead of an independently smooth line of sixteenth-notes.

The degree of shortening of staccato notes needs separate appraisal for every passage that is encountered. Legato may be simply defined as 'bound together', meaning a smooth progression with no break of sound between notes. Staccato on the contrary includes many grades of shortening, from the almost imperceptible breaks of 'portamento' (a term borrowed from singing) to the pistol-shot abruptness of staccatissimo. The term 'portamento staccato' as used by pianists implies that a note will be held for almost its full value, and then lifted at the last moment before sounding the next note. A useful test of portamento is to play a series of different but adjacent notes with the same finger, trying to hold on to each note to the last possible moment. The degree of shortening of a staccato should always blend with the overall character of a passage, and it is a common fault with students (a) to be too clipped with cadence-endings closing a tranquil section or movement, where undue abruptness, even if played quietly, can break the peaceful atmosphere rudely; and (b) to spoil a melodic passage that happens to contain detached notes by playing them in so explosively abrupt a style that at times even the melodic pitch of the notes is not clearly established. It is often stated that a staccato dot will halve the length of the sound, but this is a dangerous generalization; in some cases it may be regarded as correct, but staccato is far too subtle a thing to be defined by such a facile 'rule'.

The actual signs for staccato are: (a) the simple dot; (b) the slurred staccato (portamento) of dots covered by a slur over a group of notes; and (c) the small vertical wedge of staccatissimo, and they need an understanding with regard to the historical period of the composer using them. In Haydn's time the vertical wedge was not intended as staccatissimo at all: it must be played either as a normal staccato (with length of sound appropriate to the surrounding texture), or as a slight accent, or as a combination of accent and normal staccato. The differentiation between the wedge and the dot came in Beethoven's time; Beethoven in addition to using both the dot and the wedge to indicate staccato and staccatissimo respectively, also used the dot to suggest slight accentuation (see Op. 110, first movement, from bar 12).

Ex 151

This may be an opportune moment to mention the reverse or opposite of staccato – the 'tenuto' mark, which is the short horizontal line placed over a note or chord, implying that it must be held for its full value (or even, at times, for slightly longer than its value). The tenuto mark did not come into use until the last years of the nineteenth century, though the word 'tenuto' and its abbreviation 'ten.' were used by Beethoven. Instead of the tenuto mark it appears that composers used the horizontal accent > which, according to circumstances, would be interpreted either as a tonal accent or as an agogic accent – i.e. an indication to give the note emphasis by lingering very slightly on it. Examples from Chopin include:

Etude in C sharp minor, Op. 25, No. 7

Ex 152

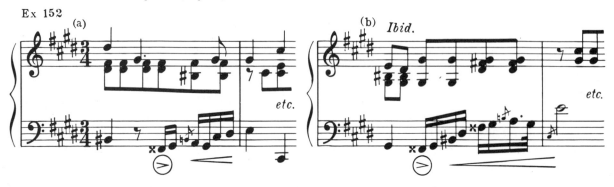

In these cases a tonal accent would be unmusical and tonally ugly. The accent, understood as a tenuto sign, suggests the freedom of a gentle rubato.

It will be readily grasped that in many movements more than one type of staccato may be found; this extends to the works of Bach. Though Bach did not mark slurs and dots, the texture of the third section of the *Sinfonia* to the C minor Partita requires more than one degree of staccato.

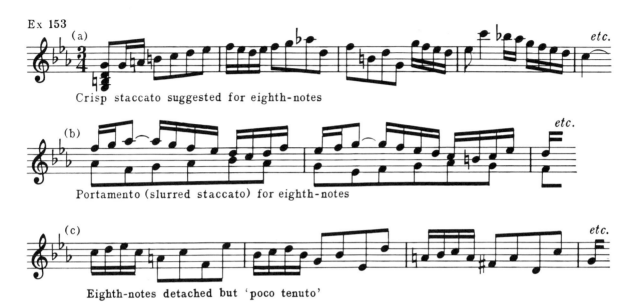

It may be noted that the general tendency with the unmarked phrases of Bach is to play conjunct movement of tones and semitones slurred, and leaping intervals detached, but one cannot make a strict rule of this, as many exceptions will be found.

We find that certain customs or conventions with regard to articulation must also be recognized in Mozart's keyboard works. Mozart is sparing in his indications and it is rare to find passage-work of sixteenth-notes in *Allegro* tempo covered by a slur. It seems appropriate therefore that in dealing with rapid passage-work in his concertos and sonatas we should use the touch sometimes known as 'jeu perlé' – every note a separate pearl! In Mozart's time it was presumed that in the absence of any indication of articulation a passage would be played 'non legato'. In passages that are intended to be legato it will be noted that Mozart generally ends his slurs before the bar-line, leaving the bars apparently unconnected; it is however to be understood that this custom probably derives from a string player's bowing technique, and certainly no break of continuity can be tolerated in a running passage that finishes a bar with a leading note, followed by the tonic coming as the next note after the bar-line.

There are innumerable such cases to be found in Haydn, Mozart and early Beethoven.

The articulation slurs in Mozart's writing which are however to be strictly observed are the short ones connecting only two notes, three notes and, very occasionally, four notes.

Piano Sonata in F, K.332                                                    Mozart

Ex 155

The phrasing of the opening subject of Mozart's Sonata in B flat, K. 570, presents pianists with something of a problem; here he writes:

Ex 156
Allegro

and this should be taken as another instance of articulation slurs suggested by a string player's change of bow; a violinist will not take his bow from the string yet his change of bow can be detected. The pianist in this case must not play the third-beat quarter-note staccato, nor should there be an even-toned legato throughout; can he, by slight accentuation on the first beat of each bar suggest a fresh impetus that swings the rhythm along as a change of bow would do? This particular subject of K. 570 does, incidentally, also need a subtle difference of tone to suggest the 'strong bar – weak bar' rhythmic alternation.

It is self-evident that 'rests' are an important feature when considering punctuation: they are the obvious breathing-places lightening the texture to let air in, and they are also used for dramatic purposes. Before the invention of the sustaining or damper pedal in the last twenty years of the eighteenth century no complication was present for keyboard players in this matter of rests: they were to be strictly observed for the exact duration as indicated by the composer. The introduction of the sustaining pedal however brought some confusion, particularly in the case of the romantic composers who exploited all the resources of the instrument, and we find Chopin, for instance, writing short quarter-note bass notes in his Second Scherzo (bars 5 and 49, and elsewhere) expecting them to be sustained by the pedal for several bars.

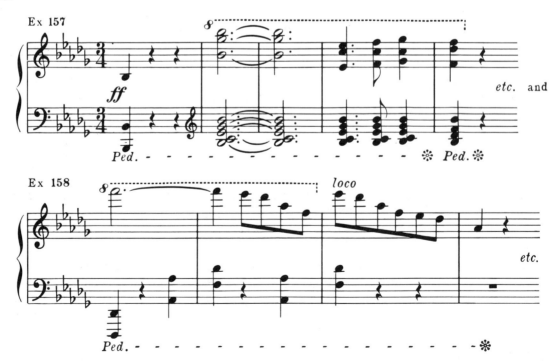

These bass notes are clearly intended to be the foundation for rich harmonic effects; the hands will lift as if playing a short quarter-note, but the pedal will certainly sustain into the fourth bar. The sustaining of such basses, though not always indicated by pedal markings, is felt to be intended when the following bars of unchanged harmony would otherwise lack a foundation. The pedal is also expected to sustain notes longer than their true value in broken-chord figures such as are found in Chopin's Etude in A flat, Op. 25, No.1.

Ex 159

We also find Beethoven writing notes of short time-value and expecting them to be sustained, but examination of facsimiles of his manuscripts shows that he was invariably careful to mark the necessary pedal signs. Beethoven, incidentally, indicated special pedal effects only, and left the normal use of the sustaining pedal to the discretion of the player.

Piano Sonata, Op. 53, (*Waldstein*) 3rd movement

Ex 160

note that the pedal must be lifted on the last rest.

From consideration of the above it is clear that the pianist must adapt his approach to this subject of rests according to the period of the music which he is playing: absolute precision with regard to rests is called for in the works of all composers up to the time of Beethoven; a different approach will be required for music written later, with the pedal taken into consideration according to the character and the texture of the passage. Woe betide the chamber-music pianist who in playing Mozart and other earlier music, holds a note whether by finger or pedal a fraction longer than is written; one's instrumental colleagues are generally trained by orchestral experience to be meticulous about such matters.

Lastly, on the subject of punctuation, the treatment of pauses (fermata) requires understanding and imagination. Whilst some pause notes require no breathing-space before proceeding to the next phrase, others will mark the end of a section with a comma before continuing. The opening bars of Beethoven's D minor Sonata, Op. 31, No. 2, contain examples of each of these two types of pause: on the fourth beat of the second bar an agitated phrase grows out of the sound and atmosphere of the pause. In the sixth bar another pause occurs: this closes a complete musical sentence, and there should be a small break of sound before commencing the next sentence in a different key.

Ex 161

In the example from Beethoven's Sonata, Op. 101 the pauses in the second and fifth bars arise spontaneously after the fading of the phrases which they follow.

Ex 162

The Sonata has opened with these phrases heard in unbroken rhythm and marked *Gesangvoll, mit innigster Empfindung* (with deepest longing). Here, later in the work, time is needed for wistful reflection on memories from the past; in the following *stringendo* all this has finally to be swept away. The line provides one of the saddest passages in music. Incidentally, when the subject of the vigorous last movement is stated we find that Beethoven has founded it on a retrograde version of the opening subject of the Sonata followed by the cadential figure in the L.H.

There can be no hard and fast rule governing the lengths of pauses. It is sometimes said that a pause will approximately double the written note-value, but this is only occasionally true, and it can be misleading. In some circumstances the pause may need to be more than double the normal value; in other cases (mostly in very slow tempi) the pause may add only a little extra value.

Pauses which interrupt rhythm and action, causing shocked silence can be highly dramatic. An arresting example is found in Chopin's Fourth Ballade in F minor, Op. 52, where towards the end (bar 202) three staccato fortissimo chords are followed by a silence; following this there are five pianissimo chords of frozen stillness before the final storm breaks. During the pause it is as if time itself is arrested, and one waits in hushed suspense. Three staccato fortissimo chords are followed by a silence, then five long pianissimo chords, before the final storm of sixteenth notes; the silence demands a pause. This pause in the silent second half of the bar is in fact the core of the climax.

Ex 163

The timing of this silent pause cannot be calculated metrically: if movement is resumed too soon, tension is not given sufficient time to build up; if delayed too long, the tension begins to evaporate. A sense of dramatic timing is vital. It is, incidentally, unforgivable in this case to hold the pedal down to sustain the last chord through this pause: the pause is placed by Chopin over the 'rest', and it indicates complete silence.

## (iii) The use of tone in moulding a phrase

Rhythm and punctuation provide the necessary framework, as we have seen, for any coherent musical thought, but it is left to tone, in all its variety, to fulfil the function of giving substance and reality to such thought. We are concerned with the piano, which has an enormous range of tone and infinite variation in the possible combinations of sounds; in the hands of an artist the piano has also unlimited subtlety in the balancing and blending of tone at all levels of intensity from pianissimo to fortissimo.

The player will realize that as piano tone is produced at a precisely-timed moment by hammers striking against strings, the sound of all notes of long time-values will die away steadily. In the case of successions of rapid notes there is no measurable loss of tone, and the matching-up of sound will be directly in accordance with the nature of the passage concerned (whether on one tone-level, or with crescendo or diminuendo); but with any slow-moving melody or chord progression the player must ensure that any new sound blends with the degree of tone remaining to the previous note or chord. It is especially important for the pianist to be in full control of quiet tone in the rounding-off of cadences. If there is to be a smooth continuity in slower passages the player will be acutely aware of the need to gauge aurally, after holding a note or chord for its full value, exactly how much of the diminishing sound is left; his success, or otherwise, in blending such sounds will be the measure of his artistry.

Piano Concerto No. 4 in G, end of 2nd movement Beethoven

In the above example the finger playing the softly-resolving note (which may be held for about four sixteenth-notes) should be prepared on the surface of the key, at a point as near the front edge of the key as may be convenient (to make use of the maximum leverage of the key). Descent into the key is to be effected by a controlled lowering of the fore-arm, wrist and hand (not a muscular striking by the finger).

It is of course true that nothing a pianist can do will alter the quantity or quality of a note once struck, but this statement calls for some qualifying comment. If a melody-note or chord of long time-value is accompanied by a tremolo, Alberti-bass*, broken-chord or other figure it can be suggested by a crescendo of the accompaniment that the melody-note (or chord) is itself increasing; and the use of the sustaining pedal also helps in the cumulative effect of the tonal build-up.

Piano Sonata, Op. 14, No. 10                                                                 Beethoven

In the matter of creating an illusion: Beethoven's Sonata in D major, Op. 10, No. 3 has a well-known instance in the first movement where, shortly after the double-bar (bars 132−3), double-octaves on A (with pause) can be made to appear to swell (legato) into the double-octave B flat a semitone higher; this, however, if successful, is a triumph of personality! Certainly no actual increase of tone can possibly occur.

* A form of accompaniment providing movement in broken-chords instead of block harmonies. Named after an eighteenth-century composer who used it frequently.

Ex 166

A great deal of influence on tone can be effected by means of the sustaining pedal; if this pedal is already down when a chord is played and sustained, all the strings of the piano will be free to vibrate, and those strings which belong to the same harmonic series as the chord which has been sounded will produce audibly strong sympathetic vibrations. This can be demonstrated by depressing silently with the fore-arm as many notes as can be covered (from elbow to finger-tips) from the lowest C upwards, then by striking a staccato forte chord of C major, without pedal, in the middle register; the silently depressed keys will be heard resonating a chord of C major spread over several octaves. What is heard are the sympathetic vibrations of strings that have not actually been struck. There is of course no question here of influencing tone that has already been produced, but if a chord is played and the pedal pressed down afterwards it is certainly possible to detect a difference in the sound as sympathetic vibrations are added to those already sounding, though in this case the extra tone will be feeble.

Before leaving this subject, an explanation of the so-called 'Bebung' may be helpful in correcting any misunderstanding. The true Bebung is only possible on the clavichord, on which instrument a tone already produced can be varied, but the term Bebung is commonly used by pianists to describe a piano effect which was used several times by Beethoven (in Op. 110 and elsewhere); this makes use of the fact that if a key is lifted only partially, the repeater mechanism of the piano action permits the hammer to fall back into a position that enables it to strike again whilst the damper is still held above and not touching the strings; the same strings may therefore be struck again quietly whilst still vibrating from the effects of the first hammer-striking. It will be clear that this adds a second sound of the same pitch to the one already produced. This effect can of course be duplicated by use of the sustaining pedal in restriking a note quietly whilst the same sound is being held by the pedal.

In consequence of the nature of piano tone in diminishing after tone-production it has often been said that 'the piano cannot sing'. Throughout the history of the piano, composers and performers alike have taken up the challenge in creating the illusion that it can 'sing' – and who would deny that many beautiful melodies of Mozart, Chopin and other composers for the piano can in fact be made to sing with great beauty of tone? Think for example of the R.H. melody from the *Romanze* of the Mozart D minor Concerto, K. 466.

Ex 167

We immediately start wondering how it can be sung on the piano. Mozart's instrumental melodies are almost exclusively vocal in inspiration and style, even though they may exceed the compass of any voice. In the example given, one seeks a certain purity of tone and line, with delicate inflexions or gradations to mould the rise and fall, but with no forcing of the 'voice'. Purity of tone and 'no forcing' mean, on the piano, reducing the percussive element of touch but, remembering that these notes must sing through against repeated chords from the orchestra, the tone needs some warmth and must certainly not be 'thin'; a 'deep' touch from the surface of the key is recommended.

In contrast to this, consider the kind of tone that is appropriate for the melody which follows the broken-chord introduction of Mozart's D minor Fantasia, K. 397 (385g).

This despairing, desolate phrase does not want a rich cantabile tone; it is cold and lonely, and that is how it should be projected to an audience.

Turning now to romantic music of the nineteenth century one must imagine the warmth of tone that is wanted for the long impassioned melodic line (commencing bar 65) that builds up to the first climax in Chopin's Scherzo No. 2 in B flat minor.

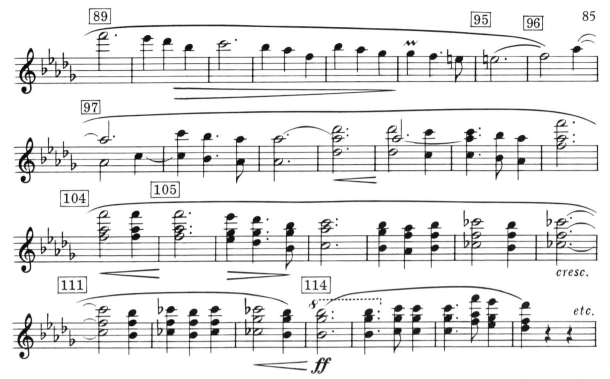

The phrases are of regular four-bar structure, but the line rises in a continuous rapture without pausing to take breath − surely one of the longest of all lines of unbroken melodic inspiration? In the first place it soars up in three stages to a first climax in bar 89 before temporarily subsiding to bars 95 − 6. Reinforced in tone by octaves, it then rises to a peak in bar 114 before coming to a triumphant close in bar 117. (Fifty-three bars of warmly romantic melody calling for all the resources of cantabile tone-production.)

In this matter of tone we can often get help from imagining what orchestral instrument might play the same passage. It is true that the piano cannot in actual fact be made to sound like a horn or a flute (nor, indeed, like any other orchestral instrument), but imaginatively it can suggest certain such qualities to us. This habit of 'thinking orchestrally' is particularly useful in many works of Beethoven, and an obvious case is found in the *Adagio* of the D minor Sonata, Op. 31, No. 2, where, from the twenty-second bar, the L.H. has an insistent timpani-like rhythm against R.H. chords that could be scored for horns.

Ex 170

Such suggestions of instrumental colouring in Beethoven are innumerable, and it is obvious that his musical thinking is primarily instrumental, from the full orchestral effects of some of his stormy middle-period piano sonatas to the more intimate subtleties of the chamber music style of the late sonatas. With Mozart all the melodies sing; with Beethoven one should think instrumentally − not forgetting however that the works these composers wrote for the keyboard can certainly be made to sound supremely effective on the modern piano.

Chopin was the special genius of the piano, and his melodies and his supporting textures show a very remarkable feeling (plus an acutely sensitive and imaginative ear) for the sheer quality of pianistic sound. A sympathetic and knowledgeable understanding of the possibilities of the sustaining pedal is essential for realization of the tonal effect of his works; and to under-pedal is as equally bad as to over-pedal (but note that very frequent changes of pedal may be necessary). Constant use of the right pedal is an integral part of the tonal effect. As an example, the following bars from the Berceuse, Op. 57 give some of the loveliest sounds of which the piano is capable; the beautiful melodic curves, 'floating' over delicately sonorous, pedalled harmonies, are enchanting.

Sounds and effects that are unique to the piano are also found in the works of Liszt; the concert study *La Leggierezza* provides a good example of rapid finger-work demanding clear articulation and delicate tonal gradations to mould the shapes of the phrases. To keep the R.H. 16th notes clear of pedal, the three notes of each L.H. harmony may be held down by the fingers.

The French composers Debussy and Ravel enlarged still further the range of sounds to be produced from the piano; typical examples are the 'watery' effects of such pieces as Debussy's *Reflets dans l'eau* and Ravel's *Jeux d'eau* – though it is likely that both of these pieces were influenced by Liszt's late and beautiful piece *Les jeux d'eaux à la Villa d'Este*.

Subtle use of tone and of pedalling is essential in much of French piano music. Many examples could be taken from Debussy and here is the opening of his Prelude *La Terrasse des audiences au Clair de Lune*.

Imagination of a high order is also found in the Prelude *Canope*, which expresses feelings aroused in contemplation of an ancient canopic jar (relic of a lost civilization – probably Egyptian). Here is the ending:

88

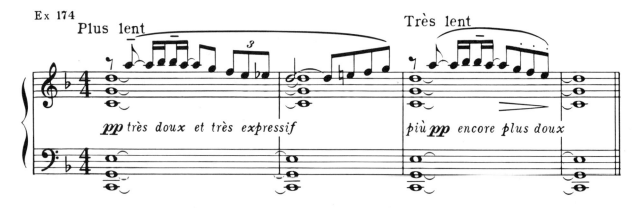

Ex 174

Ravel also shows a sensitive and highly-cultured understanding of the subtleties of the piano and technique, and the following example from his evocative piece *Ondine* is typical for its beautifully-moulded melodic line and for the delicate colouring of the supporting harmonic texture. The rising scale (pedalled) in the last bar that is quoted is magical in its effect, heard against the descending melody.

Ex 175

For a pianist the realization in appropriate sound of all the effects he is called on to produce demands a complete command of the entire tonal range of the piano:

1  He must be able to control a true whispered pianissimo that is nevertheless audible at the farthest end of a concert hall.

2  He must be able to produce a fortissimo that is an exciting sound without hardness. (Debussy has already been quoted as asking for 'sonore sans dureté'.)

3  He must be able to make gradations of tone of the most subtle nature in moulding melodic lines, and he must also be able to plan tonal effects on a grand scale, i.e. to make a crescendo that lasts for many bars (or even pages), not getting loud too soon and always saving something extra for the climax; likewise, in making a diminuendo (which is even more difficult to control than crescendo) he must be able to let the tone subside sufficiently gradually and to have something left at the end for a final irreduceable pianissimo. Examples of gradation are to be found in everything one plays: the following from Schubert's Impromptu in G flat, Op. 90, No. 3, shows a typically Schubertian 'turn' of melody which can be made into a thing of beauty:

Ex 176

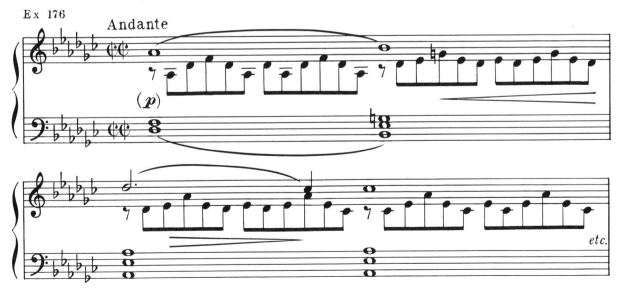

This next quotation from Mozart's Sonata in C minor, K. 457 (second movement) is an example of a build-up covering four bars; the climax is reached in the second half of the fourth bar and the augmented sixth harmony resolves into the fifth bar:

and here is a difficult diminuendo over just three bars from the sixth variation of the third movement of Beethoven's Sonata, Op. 109:

4 He must always 'have an ear' for balance of sound. This is obviously necessary in matters of melody and accompaniment, and in giving prominence to important figures in contrapuntal music. It is also vital in chord-playing: the quality and character of a chord can be altered if the constituent notes are not balanced in conformity with the general texture and style of a passage (a common fault is to have an inadequate bass as foundation for a harmonic passage).

5 Customarily, one associates the idea of climax with big tone, but do not overlook the occasions when moments of great intensity are felt in quiet passages — those rare, hushed moments when one scarcely dares to breathe lest the spell be broken.

Tone requires special consideration when playing concertos with orchestra. If one is playing one's part in combination with a particular instrument or particular section of the orchestra one needs to listen and to adjust one's tone to balance artistically, as in the second movement of Tchaikovsky's First Concerto where the balance against the cello should not make the cellist 'force' his tone.

Ex 179

At times the piano is required to challenge the full might of a symphony orchestra, and one of the most thrilling passages in all music occurs towards the end of the development section of the first movement in Beethoven's Fifth Concerto (The Emperor) where maximum power is needed for the rhythmically repeated chords which, as it were, 'cross swords' with the orchestra before dominating it in a tremendous series of octaves.

(The eventual conclusion of the octave episode presents a marvellous opportunity for a beautifully graded diminuendo.)

The piano writing of Brahms needs its own special qualities, and we find wonderfully contrasting expressive effects in the second movement of his First Concerto in D minor.

In this *Adagio*, written in memory of Robert Schumann, the first piano entry asks for gentle warmth with breadth, and with depth of feeling. The hands double each other at one octave distance, and unforced sonority and richness of tone are wanted.

The second example from the same movement comes after two bars of hushed and sombre writing for the orchestral strings, and the piano writing carries an eerie atmosphere of remote, frozen stillness that nevertheless conveys a certain wistful tenderness – a remarkable imaginative achievement for a very young composer.

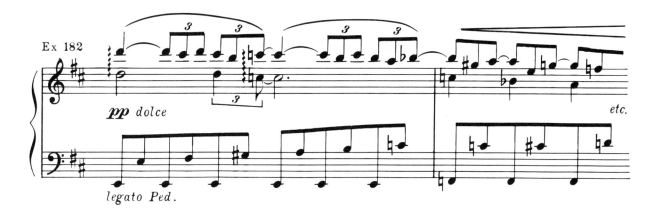

Of concerto effects one of the most imposing is the famous opening of Tchaikovsky's First Concerto:

after the two bars from the brass section the piano enters with massive chords covering practically the entire range of the keyboard (and sustained by pedal). The effect can be electrifying.

It is clear then that we must have in our minds a 'sound-ideal' that is artistically right for the period, the composer, the style and the particular musical thought that is to be expressed; and the player must have the technical equipment to respond instantly to the demands of his ear and of his imagination to produce a certain kind of tone and the right effect. Incidentally, the student is strongly recommended to stop occasionally to listen to the balance and quality of tone he has just produced, asking himself – 'is that a good sound, and is it appropriate for the type of music that is being played?'. In assessing the sound he will of course continue to hold down notes and pedal.

Before turning to give detailed consideration to a number of typical, contrasted phrases from masterpieces of the piano repertoire, it should be added that in shaping a phrase such things as accompanying harmonies and changes of accompanying patterns should also be taken into account. An unexpected harmony can throw light on how the composer regards his own themes and phrases; some of Schubert's changes of key and changes from minor to major are often sheer magic – they need discreet underlining, sometimes by playing more softly!

Impromptu, Op. 90, No. 3                                           Schubert

Ex 184

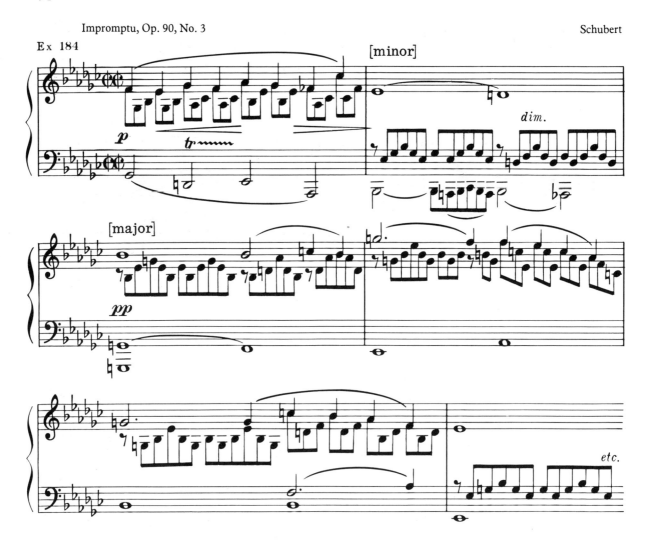

The phrases which follow have been chosen for their varied and contrasted styles; countless others could be added to the list, but it is hoped that those quoted and discussed will serve as useful models.

## (iv) Examples of phrasing

MOZART   Sonata in D major, K.576, *Adagio* movement: bars 1-16

In dealing with this theme bar by bar the intention has been to demonstrate that every note and every progression needs thought. There is indeed the danger of becoming obsessed with detail, of sounding too 'clinical' and of losing spontaneity; but a close examination of all the features of a work is to be regarded as just the first step, which should be undertaken in the early days of learning a work. To acquire insight into a masterpiece it is necessary to take infinite pains. Assimilating and absorbing every feature of a work may take considerable time, but this is unavoidable if we are eventually to reach a perspective view of it as a whole.

The opening sixteen bars of this *Adagio* from K. 576, Mozart's last sonata for piano, provide a beautifully shaped theme belonging to his maturity.

*Rhythmic character*   The melodic shapes of bars 1 and 2 (and of similar bars later) suggest clearly that in addition to the normal feeling for the first beats, the second beats of these bars need slight stress almost in the manner of a Sarabande. The last three notes of the first bar will be quietly even and smooth in completing a curve. From the ninth bar there is a change of character with the thirds of the L.H. making an independent rise and fall whilst the gently-flowing thirty-second-notes of the R.H. in bars 9 and 10 give a little prominence to the third beats in coming to a brief rest on those beats. The thirteenth bar sees a return to the opening melodic line with its slight stresses on first and second beats. The thematic pattern of these sixteen bars is A−A−B−A in regular four-bar phrases.

*Tempo*   Three slow pulses in a bar, giving a calm dignity and grace. The movement must not be so slow as to risk becoming six-in-a-bar of eighth-notes, nevertheless the tempo should allow for the turn (written-out) in the first bar to be played in unhurried style as if conceived vocally.

*Articulation*   The Urtext edition gives the authentic short slurs of the period which are intended to convey the idea of a general legato with no break in continuity in this case, until the second beat of the fourth bar. From here the legato is resumed and bars 5−8 should be played as if sung in one breath. In bars 9 and 10 the rests provide the obvious punctuation, after which bars 11 and 12 will flow smoothly into a return of the opening idea. In bar 15 the two staccato notes should be firm but not too abrupt; the wedge staccato mark of this period did not imply a clipped staccatissimo, and a normal staccato, sometimes with a degree of accentuation, is to be understood.

*Tone*   Mozart gives no tonal indications here. The style is song-like, and 'p cantabile' would seem appropriate for the opening, with gradations rising a little above that level; too soft a tone would risk a lack of sustaining power for longer notes such as the treble E in the second bar. The rise and fall of the melodic line, considered in conjunction with the rhythmic character noted above, suggest tonal gradation as follows:

Against this the cello-like bass line of quarter-notes needs careful balancing; and in the second bar the long note E is assisted in maintaining its tone by a slight crescendo of the repeated eighth-notes in the L.H. which can actually suggest an increase over the bar-line before the treble rises to A. The L.H. eighth-notes should be separately pedalled but allowed to be gently detached.

In the third bar there may be the merest suggestion of flexibility around the peak (A) of the melodic curve, but this must not interrupt the regularity of the slow quarter-note pulse. The player should then resolve the second beat E sharp quietly into F sharp, after which the rising notes at the end of this third bar may have an almost imperceptible increase of tone. The first four-bar melodic phrase ends softly on G sharp (there must be no second-beat stress in this bar). In the sixth bar there is the significant difference that the rising interval of a perfect fifth heard four bars before has here been expanded to an augmented fifth (E sharp); this requires a little more intensity (which is helped by the L.H. rising chromatically) and the melodic line lifts itself up to a modest climax. In the seventh bar sensitive treatment is needed to realize the vocal beauty of wide intervals in the second beat.

In the contrasting section starting in bar 9, the L.H. thirds will have a tendency to increase slightly in rising to the third beat, whilst simultaneously the R.H. diminishes a little in falling from D to G sharp; but bar 10 reverses these tonal gradations with R.H. increasing to a high E and the L.H. thirds falling back. It may be helpful to think of the R.H. in less decorated form:

Following this the harmonic bass falls from A to F sharp and this clearly calls for 'più p'. There may then be small gradations to outline the melodic curves in the latter parts of bars 11 and 12.

The return of the main theme on C sharp is accompanied by a dramatic change to a diminished seventh on A sharp instead of the expected tonic chord. The significance of this must not be missed, and the surprise harmony should be adequately emphasized. In the next bar (14) the melody leaps up a seventh (A to G) which compares with the previous intervals at this juncture of a perfect fifth and an augmented fifth. This, following the diminished seventh surprise, gives further dramatic intensity, and it heralds the climax of the whole sixteen-bar theme. The G natural, assisted in maintaining its tone by rising sixths in the L.H. will be joined smoothly to the following thirty-second-notes, which will be played with some breadth and fairly full (but unforced) tone. A noteworthy feature of this fifteenth bar is the two detached notes of the second beat rising strongly to the dominant before rounding-off to a calm cadence in the following bar.

The climax of this beautiful and perfectly-shaped theme is most convincingly conveyed in bars 13 – 15 by the harmonic and melodic changes to which attention has been drawn, but the texture is never thickened and remains in three-part harmony except for the contrasting bars 9 – 12. The tonal range must not be exaggerated and beautiful quality of tone should be sought throughout.

The sustaining pedal may be used discreetly with the object of adding warmth of tone, but it must not be allowed to mar the clarity and purity of the melodic line. There is no occasion in this section of the movement for the use of the *una corda* left pedal.

The L.H. should be regarded as if it were an accompaniment of strings, which would be cello and viola, with an extra part for bars 8 – 12, each part being a thing of beauty in its own right. In bar 8 the three eighth-notes of the bass should sound like a cellist taking separate bows; and in bar 13 note the expressive chromaticism of the inner (viola) part.

Aural attention needs to be acute throughout, and physical control of tone production must be such that no notes are too loud nor too soft to fit into their context; there must be perfect matching and blending of sound.

BEETHOVEN  Sonata in C major, Op.2, No.3, second movement: *Adagio* in E major: bars 1–10 resolving into the eleventh bar.

The key of E major (mediant major) shows already in this early sonata Beethoven's interest in exploiting a wide range of key-relationships by using keys a major third away from his 'home' key. A great dramatic moment in this E major movement occurs in bar 53 when Beethoven reaffirms the key of C major with a fortissimo statement of the opening figure of this movement.

*Tempo*  A slow two-in-a-bar, though in the third and fourth bars the fully-harmonized sixteenth-notes give more activity and suggest a pulse of four-in-a-bar of eighth-notes.

*Articulation and rhythmic character*  A striking feature of this theme is that it is composed entirely of short statements punctuated by rests (see also Beethoven's Sonata in E flat, Op. 7, *Largo* movement). The player must 'think' through the rests in building an eloquent theme from these separate elements, and he must avoid abrupt endings to the eighth-notes preceding the rests; tone should fade away leaving the listener awaiting the continuation of the phrases. The rhythmic figure of the opening bars

Ex 187

at once gives a dignity and solemnity to the movement. For the detailed articulation of this figure note that the thirty-second-note is not slurred to the following note; the effect should be approximately that of a string player's change of bow. The sixteenth-notes with staccato dots need good singing tone and should only be slightly shortened. This theme consists of two four-bar phrases and it is extended by adding two bars. The first of these is a repeat of syncopated progressions and the second introduces a new melodic line to complete the theme.

*Tone* The player will at once note that this theme is placed in a richly resonant part of the instrument; and the tone, though 'piano', must have a well-balanced sonority. It is necessary also to observe the falling contour of the opening two bars:

Ex 188

and a slight diminuendo will help to outline this descending line. Bars 5 and 6 repeat this line one step higher and should be given a little more intensity. In bar 3 the rising line with separate harmonies for each note will have a tendency to increase and bar 4 will be quietly resonant with a good supporting bass. At the end of bar 6 the syncopated chord coming in before the beat, as if impatient (and a little agitated), requires firm tone at a modest level; the resolutions of the syncopations will be quiet and slightly more abrupt than the other phrase-endings of this theme. The legato eighth-notes of bar 8 will have a calming influence. The syncopated progressions when repeated in the L.H. will be a little more prominent than the quietly-singing R.H. octaves. In bar 10 the final recitative-like phrase sums up in concentrated style the appeal of this opening subject; and the unaccompanied notes need generous singing tone before the diminuendo into the somewhat menacing second thematic idea of this movement.

BEETHOVEN   Sonata in C minor, Op.13 (*Pathétique*), second movement: *Adagio* in A flat: bars 1–8.

This theme is a true Beethoven utterance of noble and grave beauty. The slow movement of the *Pathétique* Sonata opens with a deservedly famous melody which maintains an unbroken legato until the portamento sixteenth-notes of the seventh bar.

*Tempo*  A slow two-in-a-bar. The player should beware playing this movement too fast, which would cause a loss of dignity and solemnity. The accompanying sixteenth-notes should have the rhythmic regularity and inevitability of Haydn's *Clock* Symphony, though at a slightly faster tempo than Haydn's ticking clock. Granted such evenness, it follows that a sensitive shaping of the melody line must be accomplished by subtle use of tone; rubato in this case would be inappropriate.

*Structure*  The formal shape of this eight-bar theme must be noted. Despite the soaring phrase of eighth-notes in the third bar the climax of intensity is felt on the first note of the fifth bar; here F in the treble is heard over a quietly sonorous D flat in the bass. From here the tone gradually subsides in a series of three falling fifths (the last of these delayed by decorative sixteenth-notes). It is a little unusual to find the climax of a classical melody coming so early as the fifth bar, i.e. at the beginning of the second four-bar phrase, and it is an arresting discovery to find that this particular shape of theme is repeated in the next movement of this sonata. In both movements one finds opening eight-bar themes with climax coming at the beginning of the fifth bar on the sixth note (sub-mediant) of the scale, and in both cases the manner of departing from the climax is by falling fifths.

Ex 189    3rd movement

As the tempo of the Rondo is a brisk *alla breve* the speeds of the two movements are vastly different. It is interesting to note that the Rondo theme begins with a rising figure which has been used in the first movement; and it will be observed that an important episode in A flat in the middle of the Rondo is built on falling fifths clearly derived from the Adagio (fifth, sixth and seventh bars) and from the opening theme of the Rondo (fifth and sixth bars).

Ex 190

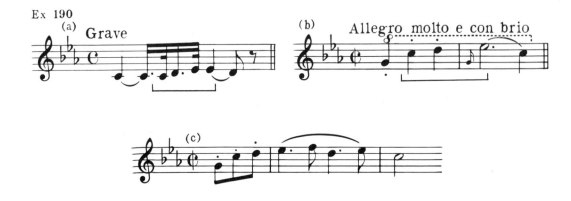

(d)

Here, it would seem, are instances, and early ones at that, of the thematic unity which pervades many of Beethoven's works.

*Tone* This theme is 'placed' in a rich part of the piano's compass to provide the maximum sonority using only a moderate level of tone. The obvious difficulty to be mastered is for the R.H. to be able to combine a warm singing tone for the melody whilst simultaneously playing a very soft supporting accompaniment of sixteenth-notes, which will, however, like a good accompanist, give support to any rise and fall of the melody line. The L.H. bass will be carefully balanced to provide a firm root for the harmony, and in falling to a lower octave in the fourth and fifth bars more resonance is given to the climax.

MOZART   Sonata in C minor, K.457, first movement: bars 1–4.

BEETHOVEN   Sonata in D minor, Op.31, No.2, first movement: bars 21–4

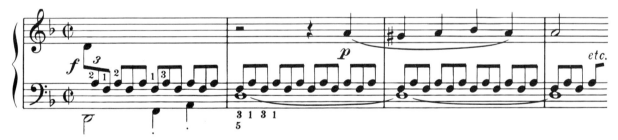

These examples are quoted together because they share the not uncommon feature of being 'Duo subjects'. In both cases a strong threatening figure rises from the bass, and is answered by a contrasting quiet but expressive phrase in the treble. Two characters are suggested, and the performer needs to be able to 'act' both of them convincingly.

Little detailed comment is necessary: in the Mozart it is recommended that after the sixteenth-note anacrusis the short trill should in this case begin on the principal note E flat; if started on the upper note the effect would be of the trill starting a sixteenth-note too early. In the third and fourth bars the repeated quarter-notes must not be staccato.

For the Beethoven example note again the duo character of bass and treble, and that the accompanying triplet eighth-notes must be played with rhythmic precision; they must not become a free tremolo. The long tied D in the bass clef will of course be held throughout by the L.H. fifth finger.

SCHUBERT   Sonata in A major, Op.120, D.664: bars 1–8.

*Tempo*   This should be such that a lively but steady four-in-a-bar is established at the opening. It should not be so fast that there is any danger of feeling this theme as an *alla breve* movement, yet sufficiently flowing that the octaves in the development section have a touch of bravura and virtuosity.

*Rhythmic character*   In this theme it is interesting to note that activity in the melodic line is almost entirely given to the second halves of the bars, though the L.H. maintains a constant movement of quiet accompanying eighth-notes. It is a characteristic of this melody that in bars 1, 3, 5 and 7 the last two eighth-notes have an independent life that suggests slight stressing as if these eighth-notes had separate syllables in a vocal line:

Ex 191

and it may be noted that in bars 1 and 5 the last eighth-notes (both C sharps) of these bars are foreign to the underlying harmony.

*Articulation*   This is straight-forward in requiring unbroken legato except for the rests in the fourth and seventh bars.

*Tone*   'piano' is marked in the Urtext and is presumably Schubert's indication; for the R.H. a good singing quality is required, and tone must certainly not be 'thin'. As mentioned above, a hint of emphasis may be given to the last two eighth-notes of bars 1, 3, 5 and 7. In bar 2 the eighth-notes are 'linking' notes only and should commence 'pp'; there may then be a 'poco crescendo'. The second half of the theme will commence 'piano', but note the A sharp of the L.H. which with its harmony takes us into B minor, and as the bass rises there is a crescendo into the sixth bar. The bass (dominant E) brings us back to A major, and the melody after reaching out to a high F sharp (which merits a suspicion of a 'tenuto') closes the whole phrase gracefully and quietly on the tonic.

In the third and seventh bars Schubert marks staccato dots for the first notes of the L.H. bass groups: it is presumed that these apply only to the lift of hand necessary to find the next notes, and that pedal will in fact sustain these basses. A further point is that for the majority of hands it will be necessary to spread the R.H. chords of the first bar and the third-beat chord of the seventh bar; the best effect will be to sound the two lower notes of the R.H. simultaneously with the L.H. bass. The two notes making an up-beat to the first bar must be rhythmically precise, with the D an exact sixteenth-note proceeding up to E; this is difficult for a small hand to manage neatly.

SCHUBERT   Impromptu in A flat, Op.142, No.2: bars 1–4.

The opening phrase of this Impromptu provides a good example of the subtle differences in tonal values that are possible within the simple rhythm of 'three-four' time.

Bar 1, which repeats the chord of A flat on the second beat, requires (at pianissimo level) a slight stressing of this second beat in addition to the normal firmness given to the first beat. No note is struck on the third beat.

In bar 2 the melodic A flat is a dissonance of the seventh over the bass B flat, and it should resolve with fractionally less tone on the G natural of the second beat; but the supporting harmony repeats the rhythmic pattern of the first bar and would therefore seem to require a similar slight stress on this second beat. These two apparently conflicting claims must be reconciled, and it is suggested that, to keep the rhythmic pattern clear, there should be separate articulation of both melody and harmony for these first two beats of the bar; there should however be a little less tone on the second beat in accordance with the needs of the resolving A flat of the melody.

The third bar has three even slurred quarter-notes. The treble, in sequence, again quietly resolves a dissonant seventh (B flat down to A flat), but here the third beat is for the first time separately harmonized and needs its own special value in leading onwards with a small tonal increase to the C of the fourth bar.

This opening phrase needs careful and sensitive consideration but the final effect should be that of spontaneous simplicity.

For further evidence of the rhythmic and tonal subtleties that are possible within simple triple time the reader should refer to Brahms' Waltzes of Op. 39. Brahms varies and contrasts the styles and characters of these Waltzes with great ingenuity and resource, exploiting rhythmic patterns which have a wide range of different stresses.

CHOPIN Nocturne in D flat, Op.27: bars 1–6.

This Nocturne, one of the most poetic of the whole series, begins with an exquisite melody line which appears to float on a gentle sea of D flat resonance. The L.H. figure which supplies this harmonic background is an extension of the old Alberti-bass, with wider compass now made possible by use of the sustaining pedal. The L.H. sixteenth-notes continue unbroken throughout the piece. As with many of Chopin's works this accompanying figure should be kept as even and regular as possible to produce an almost hypnotic effect; meanwhile the decorations of the R.H. must 'sing' with apparent freedom.

*Tempo* The opening and final pages of this Nocturne suggest the rhythmic movement of a lullaby (parts of the middle of the piece are too impassioned to continue this analogy). The tempo will therefore be a slow two in a bar.

*Articulation* In these opening bars there will be an unbroken legato in the R.H. melody except for some ambiguity in bar 4; when bar 28 repeats this phrase note-for-note Chopin gives the following slurs of articulation:

In bar 4 these notes are included in one slur. The questions that each player has to decide for himself are (a) is it intended that the phrase will be simple on the first occasion, and broken (therefore a little restless) at the second hearing? or (b) is it merely capricious to consider altering the articulation of a passage which has the same accompaniment and equally quiet tone in each of the bars concerned? If this latter view is held, then bar 4 should have the same treatment as bar 28. (It is illuminating to recall that Bach, who rarely gave articulation marks, also slurred falling fourths in bars 111 to 114 of his D major Toccata.)

Ex 193

*con discrezione*

*Tone*  The L.H. requires a good foundation of a first-beat D flat (but tone not more than 'p') after which the inner notes of the accompanying figure will, in the opening bars, be 'pp'. The R.H. melody must have a good cantabile quality and Chopin's marking of 'p dolce' will be observed. Care will be needed in the second half of bar 2 (R.H.) to ensure that the D flat has fractionally less tone than the preceding E flat. In the third bar there will be a hint of breadth as the rising sixteenth-notes soar up to the peak B flat in the next bar. This B flat will resolve quietly into A flat, and the falling phrase from here may have a hint of rubato freedom. The A natural of the next bar must have sufficient tone to sing through to its resolution in the next bar.

If the L.H. is played with a perfectly controlled soft tone the sustaining pedal may be held through without changing from the beginning to the fifth bar where the harmony changes. The player will be listening intently to balance throughout and if L.H. tone tends to be cumulative he should resort to occasional 'flutter' pedalling in order to reduce any unwanted resonance, but on no account should the harmony be damped completely within these early bars. The first (bass) notes of the L.H. groups may have slightly more tone than the inner notes.

Bars 10–17 (same work).

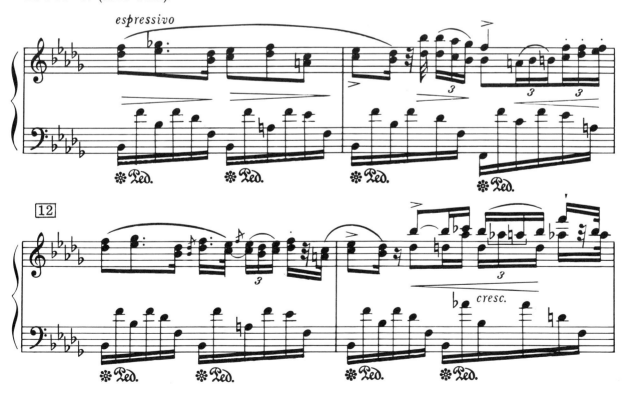

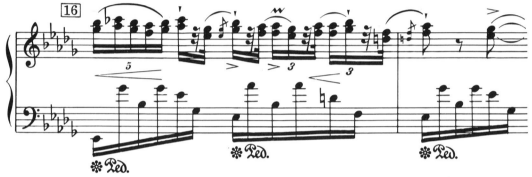

It is important to note that the richly-ornamented passages starting at bar 10 consist of two-bar phrases: two in B flat minor (relative minor) leading (via the second half of bar 13) to E flat minor in the next bar. There is a feeling of gradually mounting tone and emotional tension leading away from the idyllic peace of the opening (but the tranquillity is to return in bar 26, and the climax of the piece is to come later in bars 55–63). Contrasting with the single-note melody of the first nine bars, this next section is all in double-notes (in the R.H.), and it is necessary to ensure that good singing prominence is given to the upper notes. There is a rhapsodic quality here which demands a degree of freedom, but this element of rubato must be contained within the two steady pulses which are the rhythmic foundation of the Nocturne; and the regularity of the L.H. must not be interrupted. This need for freedom in expressive decorative melodic passages whilst maintaining a steady rhythmic background is one of the major problems to be solved in the artistic presentation of Chopin's works.

Bar 10 starts softly but there is a crescendo leading to a slightly firmer and more elaborate repeat of the phrase in bar 12. Another crescendo (bar 13) on a written-out treble 'turn' leads to the new key a fourth higher, where there are further repeats of the same basic figure (in thirds). Detailed points to note include: in bar 11 (and also 15) a short thirty-second-note is called-for following the brief rest, then a hint of tenuto licence for the first of the triplet sixths which will enhance the appeal of this phrase. Also in bar 11 the inner chromatic sixteenth-notes may be played rubato, slightly holding back the first two or three, before moving forward into the next bar. In bar 12 the rest before the end of the bar produces the effect of an emotional 'catch' in the voice; the grace-notes in this bar should fall on the beat and not before it. Bar 13: the upper part is to be regarded as a free 'turn' (in this the C flat should not be too small in tone).

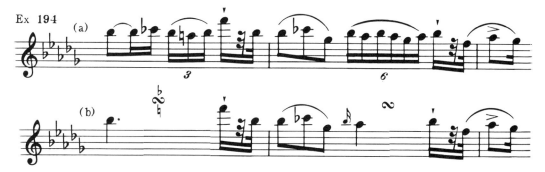

Bar 14: the second half of the bar presents another free 'turn' on A flat (in thirds) preceded by an appoggiatura. In bar 16 the sign ∿ should not be interpreted as a banal triplet but performed as if:

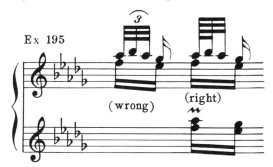

To prevent blurring of the R.H. it will often be necessary to change pedal: this presents a problem as the harmonic support of the L.H. cannot be lost. It is recommended that the inner notes of the L.H. should generally be held down here with the fingers, and the device of half-pedalling will be frequently used to sustain the bass notes which mark the half bars. Great skill in pedalling is called-for, and the right foot must respond instantly to the demands of the ear.

CHOPIN   Barcarolle, Op.60: bars 71–82.

One of the outstanding passages of this supreme example of romantic music is found in Chopin's 'bridge' from the end of his middle section in A major back to F sharp major (the tonic key) where he returns to his first subject. What in the hands of many composers is an awkward 'seam' to be masked as convincingly as possible by good craftsmanship becomes with Chopin a centre-point of the work and a thing of beauty in itself.

The modulating passage of bars 72–78 is subtle and expressive. Emotionally it brings us gradually down from the peak of ecstasy which has been reached in the immediately preceding bars; but first, the whole-bar trill suggests tension in its rise from E to F sharp. The F sharp does, as it were, attempt to maintain its pitch despite changing harmonies below which are based on the root E; but eventually it cannot as a major ninth (F sharp over E) hold that position any longer and it falls to F natural (as a minor ninth). After this, with the bass slipping down from E, through D natural, to C sharp, the F natural enharmonically becomes E sharp and we find the harmony firmly established as the dominant of our 'home' or tonic key of F sharp major. The linking modulation is accomplished.

During the three bars following the trill on E, the bass (with staccatos marked for each bar) has become faintly uneasy and troubled, hinting at something ominous, and in the fourth bar after the trill there is not a single one of the four beats in the bar which does not sound a falling note; everything that is held dear is slipping away. Relief from the unrest is found with the establishment of the C sharp major harmony, and now commences one of Chopin's most inspired passages. For this he uses the Italian term 'sfogato' which may be translated as vaporous or misty: the aim should be to produce an effect of unreality.

Similarly as with the bars from the Berceuse quoted in Ex. 171, Chopin here creates the opportunity for some of the most exquisite sounds that can be drawn from a piano; there is a beautifully undulating melody line that soon soars to a peak before falling, and it is supported by a soft 'wash' of pedalled harmony. One is living momentarily in a dream-world conjured up by the imaginative genius of the already mortally ill composer – yet one is aware that this transcendent music carries more than a hint of wistful sadness, as if dimly knowing that such ecstasy can never become reality.

Sensitive pedalling is needed to produce the atmospheric effect suggested by 'sfogato'. It is also necessary to give much thought to the shaping and scanning of the melodic curves of the R.H. In each of the four bars (78–81) the L.H. supplies an harmonic background of arpeggios with a quiet but firm bass which should be sustained by pedal until almost the end of each bar; this implies holding the pedal through various R.H. melodic notes, but such pedalling is justified by the placing of the R.H. high in the treble and by the fact that the tonal level is 'piano' with only delicate gradations to mould the phrases. Suggestions for the scanning are given (in square brackets), but there must be no break in the legato.

Incidentally, in bar 78 the first of the eighth-notes should not be played until the L.H. arpeggio is complete. It will no doubt have been observed that the most important melodic motif used here, and throughout the work, is the following simple arched figure (which has many variations):

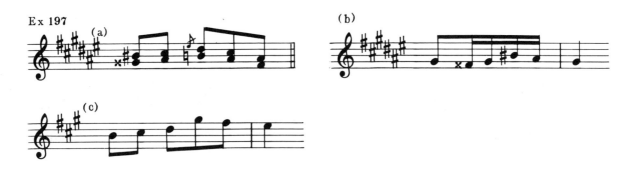

BRAHMS  Intermezzo in A major, Op.118: bars 57–62 (più lento).

There are rare occasions when the pianist must be able to produce level and even pianissimo tone without inflection, and one such passage occurs in the middle 'più lento' section of this Intermezzo.

Written towards the end of his life this Intermezzo, like several others of the same period, is wistfully nostalgic (Brahms uses the term *teneramente* a number of times in these late pieces). In this particular passage, in F sharp major, chords in both hands gently outline a canon (does the 'endless' canon suggest the dreamer's mind focussed on one memory and, as it were, going round in circles?). From the fifth bar of this passage a quiet but disturbing A natural creeps in, and after a pause there is a return to a minor version of the same melodic figure, now more passionate.

For each chord the fingers will be prepared on the surface of the keys; there will be a small rise and fall of the wrist conveying fore-arm movement to the fingers. At the timed instant of sound-production there will be a momentary muscular contraction; controlled key-speed must ensure that tone is perfectly matched, and as soft as possible.

Bars 76–84 (same work).

The outstanding emotional moment of this Intermezzo occurs in bars 81–82. The opening figure of the piece

**Ex 198** (a)

leaps up from B to A (a seventh higher) as if reaching out to something that is unattainable. Four times this recurs, always to be frustrated (the figure is even inverted in bars 33–5).

(b)

After the middle section of the Intermezzo the opening figure returns yet again, at first without success, leading to an angry rinforzando passage, then at last (and once only) the rising seventh becomes an octave, and it is as if the clear memory (which for so long had eluded him) of something precious that happened long ago is for a brief moment recaptured with infinite tenderness. It is suggested that the high melody-note B is taken softly and *molto dolce*.

These late pieces of Brahms surely present some of the most personal and most touching moments in the whole of music. One feels to be eavesdropping on Brahms' most intimate thoughts.

BRAHMS   Rhapsody in E flat, Op.119: bars 1–10.

This is Brahms' last work for piano, and the opening is unusual in being built on a series of five-bar phrases. That, at any rate, is the initial appearance of the passage from the placing of the bar-lines; but one finds in the first three phrases (of five bars each) a certain ambiguity. Noting the accents covering various chords, one realizes that the aural effect cuts across the bar-lines, and we are in fact listening to two bars in $\frac{2}{4}$ time followed by two bars in $\frac{3}{4}$ time, making a four-bar phrase with changing numbers of beats per bar.

From bar 16 the phrases are of true five-bar length (subdivided 3 + 2). The ambiguous pattern returns at bar 41. The A flat middle section (grazioso) is also unusual, commencing with eight-bar phrases which have the subdivisions 3 + 2 + 3; as the last two subdivisions are joined in continuous legato eighth-notes the effect to the listener is of 3 + 5.

The pianissimo C major section (bar 153) also has five-bar phrases which have the same scanning as the opening of the work. The whole work is full of rhythmic interest and has enormous vitality. It is absolutely necessary that the player should be aware of what is happening rhymthically if this Rhapsody is to be played with conviction and understanding.

RACHMANINOV Concerto No.2 in C minor: second subject, starting ten bars after figure 4 in miniature score.

This is given as an example of a theme which unfortunately runs out of steam before its course is run. It rises up splendidly, and with warmth, to the second beat of the second bar which would appear to be both the tonal and emotional peak of this ten-bar subject. The phrase is well-rounded as far as the fifth bar, after which the composer falls back on a sequential repetition followed by a somewhat lame tail-piece (for the latter two bars of which the violas and clarinet provide a cadential counterpoint).

114

The player must show involvement in rising up with his tone at the opening in an emotional gush; the L.H. which rises over two octaves here supports the melody admirably. From the peak A flat care is needed to avoid too rapid a diminuendo in subsiding through the sequences with their touch of lush chromaticism down to the seventh bar.

RACHMANINOV   Concerto No.3 in D minor: opening theme.

A more distinguished theme than that quoted from the Second Concerto is given above. This long theme is extraordinarily well put together and built up; in using mainly intervals moving by step it is possible that it reflects subconsciously Rachmaninov's admiration for the great theme of the final movement of Beethoven's Choral Symphony which he is known to have considered the most perfect of melodies. Rachmaninov's slurring and his gradations convey his directions for performance with admirable clarity.

DEBUSSY   Reflets dans l'eau: bars 1–4, and 9–10.

These bars are quoted as contrasting examples of pedalling in Debussy's style of piano writing; also note the use of rubato over two-bar periods, and the need to prepare and to control to pianissimo level the quickly-changing hand-positions of the R.H. three-part chords.

Debussy's time-signature of $\frac{4}{8}$ (instead of $\frac{2}{4}$) indicates a tempo considered in relation to eighth-notes (though this does not hold throughout the piece). The rubato indicated is understood as implying flexibility in lingering very slightly at the beginning on the first two or three eighth-notes, then moving gently forward until there is a little slackening towards the end of the second bar. This general pattern of rubato holds for the first eight bars.

The use of the sustaining pedal is a vital factor in producing the tonal effects of this piece. With the pedal pressed down before starting (in order to secure the maximum resonance from the first bass notes) there is then no need to lift the pedal until the last notes of the second bar. The three-note chords of the R.H. are superimposed over the sustained bass. Some pianists may prefer changing the pedal for the second and third R.H. sixteenth-note chords, but with Debussy's pianissimo to be observed this is not altogether necessary. In these opening phrases the pedal need only be changed every two bars; the *una corda* however should be held throughout this section. Note that with regard to tone the horn-like quarter-notes marked with tenuto will be made gently prominent with a slight stress on F and diminishing a little to the E flat.

From bar 9 the fundamental harmonies changing with each sixteenth-note require separate pedalling, with the legato harmonies as clearly damped as in classical playing. The top notes of the chords must be heard clearly, and the chromatic bass octaves will support the poco crescendo. The descending sixteenth-notes in the high treble should be as soft as possible as if coming from a distance.

RICHARD RODNEY BENNETT  Scena 1

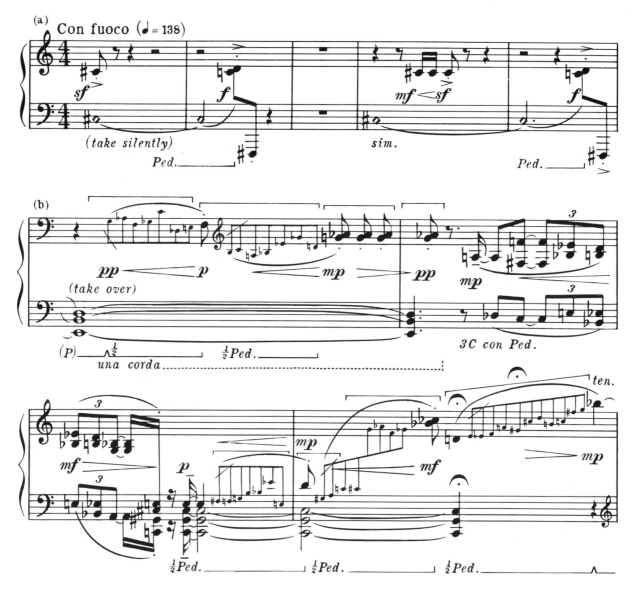

WILFRID MELLERS  Natalis Invicti Solis

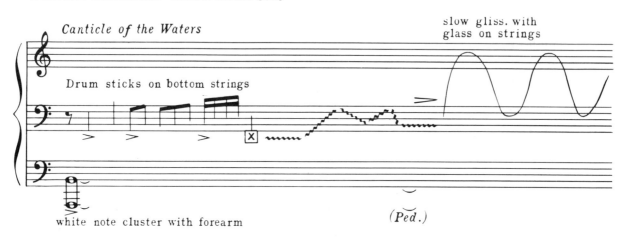

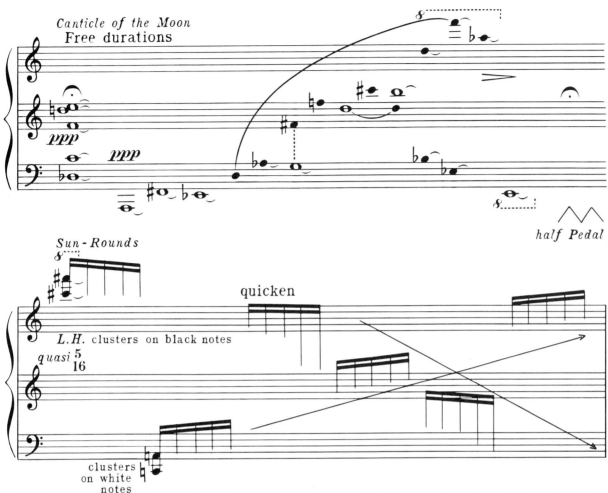

With contemporary piano music one finds the composers of to-day experimenting with novel – and sometimes bizarre – effects to be obtained from the piano. These are not confined to normal use of the keyboard, and often a preliminary list of instructions is necessary, including explanations of the symbols or signs which are used in addition to normal notation.

The examples given here are modest in their demands. Richard Rodney Bennett lists only the following extensions of classical notation: diamond-shaped notes to be taken silently and resonated by vigorous striking of another note. In this case the diamond-shaped note is C sharp in the bass clef to be resonated by its octave C sharp in the middle of the keyboard. He also uses groups of grace-notes which are to be articulated rapidly and lightly within square brackets which indicate quarter-note value. It will be noted in the second example which is quoted that half-pedalling is required for the grace-note groups; this is puzzling and it is likely that he is asking for what is more generally known as half-damping (see comments on pedalling in Chapter II). The piece is well-constructed and clear in its texture.

In the first of the four pieces which comprise Wilfrid Mellers' imaginative suite *Natalis Invicti Solis* the composer indicates that drum sticks are to be used directly on the bottom strings of the piano, followed by a slow glissando with glass, also on the strings. In the second piece the pianist should improvize a coda, and he requires an assistant to operate electronic amplification at the end of the movement. In the third piece (*Canticle of the Moon*) the duration of the notes is in some passages left to the discretion of the performer; and in the final number (*Sun-Rounds*) clusters of notes on both black and white keys are to be played with increasing speed, whilst towards the end the player is asked to improvize a cadenza using both the flat of the hand and the fist for note-clusters, and ending with a tremolo.

CHAPTER V

# Analysis and imagination

It may seem a little odd to combine analysis and imagination, which might appear to be in opposition, in one chapter. Musical analysis is sometimes regarded as a somewhat dry academic exercise doing little more than to 'describe' the external features of a movement ('the second subject starts in bar 'xy' in the key of 'z' minor . . . ') and attempting little or nothing in the way of searching for its inner meaning or motivation. Imagination, on the other hand, is capable of any flight of fancy within the medium of the art concerned. In a performing art such as piano-playing, which is concerned with the realization or recreation of the composer's aims or 'message', an imagination which is given free rein could lead one badly astray if there is any uncertainty or lack of knowledge about the background, the style and the structure of a work.

Robert Schumann wrote: 'Only when the form is clear to you can the spirit speak clearly' (or words in German to that effect). If one agrees with Schumann, then analysis and imagination are indivisibly linked and interdependent. A detailed analysis can help the performer to grasp the inner logic and architecture of a composition, and it may lead him, with the help of intuition and of informed imagination, to an understanding of the composer's vision. The value of analysis to the serious performer cannot be exaggerated.

Analysis of a musical work can be made from different angles. Normal text-book analysis divides a work into sections; if we consider sonata first-movement form it is undoubtedly convenient to tabulate, as points of reference, the exposition, development, recapitulation and coda, but such things tell us little about the way the composer's mind was working. It becomes a little more searching to note thematic groupings, key-schemes and relative lengths of sections, and these aspects can lead us nearer to our goal of obtaining an insight into the composer's aims; but to arrive at a deeper understanding and a feeling for the inner meaning and unity of a masterpiece it is necessary (a) to make a close examination of the evolution and relationships of the thematic material with which the composer has chosen to work; (b) to appreciate the time-scale on which he is working (the time element in music shows enormous range from perfect miniatures such as some of Chopin's Preludes, to the Beethoven *Eroica* Symphony or Ninth Symphony, and on to the vast length of a Wagner music-drama − not that the longest works are necessarily the greatest); and, with the appropriate time-scale in mind, to try to attain a perspective grasp of the relative values and tensions of a work, noting such contrasting factors as (i) building up to a climax over a long period and subsiding from it in a way which will balance the structure, or (ii) any sudden dramatic changes such as we find in the first movement of Beethoven's Sonata in E major, Op. 109, bar 9.

The function of an analysis in depth would seem to be in some measure a reversal of the creative art (and science) of musical composition. The composer will, in commencing a work, have a more or less clear idea of the scope and the style of the work he intends to write, and from that point he labours to find the outward means of expressing his thoughts (and perhaps his emotions also) in coherent, organized sound. The one who analyses his work can only hear the finished composition and examine the score and, from those external expressions of the composer's thoughts can try to find why the work was written in just that way, hoping to get some understanding of what was in the composer's mind. This, as stated above, is a kind of working backwards in attempting to get at the roots of inspiration. The matter becomes complicated and involved and difficult to fathom when, as is sometimes the case, the composer himself may not have been fully aware of the motivations that compelled him to write a work precisely in the way that he did. The unconscious or subconscious working of the mind in musical creativity is a fascinating subject for the musical psychologist.

Touching on this aspect of creative composition one marvels at the way in which Beethoven on occasion appears to have had a vision of a whole vast movement before the themes he was to use in it were clear in his mind; his note-books, particularly those relating to the *Eroica* Symphony, give evidence of this. The well-known critic Ernest Newman wrote of the first movement of that symphony: 'We get the impression that in some extraordinary way the movement possessed him as a whole before he began to think out the details'. Far from inventing musical themes and then proceeding to develop them, he had some kind of inspired conception of the shape and of the effect the work must have and, with certain salient features of the architecture of this wonderful movement already firmly established in his mind, he worked back to the practical matter of finding the notes that were to express what he had to say, painfully and laboriously chiselling out the themes and details of treatment – much as a sculptor may see a statue 'locked-up', as it were, in a raw block of marble. This vision of a movement that was to break new ground in the history of music reveals imagination of the highest order; and from that peak of creative imagination in composition we can more humbly ask ourselves what is the scope of imagination in performance?

The Concise Oxford Dictionary definition of the verb 'to imagine' is: 'To form a mental image of . . .'. This definition applied to piano performance implies that one is imagining the tone that is artistically right, imagining the nuance of a phrase that is to be played, imagining the poetic or expressive idea behind the notes and trying to convey it, imagining the structure of the piece as a whole – imagination does in fact embrace every aspect of performance.

This comprehensive understanding of imagination is worth stressing, as a more limited view is sometimes taken. Recently, one candidate for a diploma examination, answering a question about differences of style in playing works by Beethoven, Debussy and other composers, wrote quite acceptably on the picturesque quality of Debussy's impressionism in his *Images* and Preludes; then turning his attention to Beethoven wrote bluntly: 'As far as I am aware there is no pictorial element in Beethoven's compositions, therefore imagination is not one of the qualities called for in playing his works'. Such naïvety is hard to credit. Whilst not commenting on the debatable statement that there is no pictorial element in any of Beethoven's work, it is obvious that musical imagination covers a great deal more ground than the conjuring up before the mind's eye more or less vivid pictures of 'gardens in the rain' or 'submerged cathedrals', admirable though these latter are in their own right.

For the performer, does it not require a much greater effort of imagination and also of intellect to attempt to grasp the message of such works as Op. 109, 110 and 111? The ultimate aim of the serious performer should be to acquire an intellectual, emotional and, when applicable, a spiritual understanding of a masterpiece in the way that he imagines the composer conceived it; then to find through his own personality and technique the means of projecting and communicating his convictions about the work to his audience. He must realize, and constantly remind himself, that in their finest works the great composers were living their lives in terms of music – their most vivid experiences of life found their expression in sound. The performer must consequently call, without sparing himself, on his own vitality and imagination, and on his own experience of life, in his attempt to recreate all the vitality and experience that the composer wrote into his work. The music must be brought to life at every performance, the sound imagined afresh every time – the ideal should be to give every performance the freshness of a 'first performance' yet presented with the knowledge and confidence that can only come from long experience.

With a great work one can spend much time learning the notes, finding out all one can about its place in the composer's life, analysing the form and texture – and still be without an inner awareness of its deeper significance; then how rewarding it can be when suddenly in a flash the real problem that the composer is concerned with – the real truth – dawns upon one. Sometimes it seems that knowledge, reasoning and analysis will not of themselves yield what one imagines to be the innermost secrets of a great work of art, and that intuition is left to make the final leap. Nevertheless, it is the patient preparation which forms a sound base from which the intuitive leap can be made. It is only the amateur who may feel that facts fetter him (and who says that he 'likes to play as he feels'). The true artist is prepared to go to endless trouble in his reading, his reasoning, his practising – hoping he may be fortunate enough to have an occasional moment of true enlightenment.

To sum up on this aspect: an understanding of any great work must be based on as much solid fact about it as can be gathered; the eventual and the essential aim of analysis and of imagination is to attempt to understand and to feel about the work as nearly as possible as the composer himself must have done. 'Imagination is good but it must always be controlled by the critical facts' – so wrote Albert Einstein, the great mathematician and scientist. May it be repeated that it is essential to have an informed imagination.

Turning now to consider some other aspects of imagination: there is the difficulty of forming a conception of any big musical work, any long movement as a whole. If one were considering a painting it would be possible to stand back to see the relationship of the parts to the whole. As this is not possible with music the nearest equivalent should be to play through long sections, and then the whole work complete, frequently. We must make a judgment as to the relationship of the parts of a work to the whole, assessing the relative significance of the various sections; we must judge the relative strengths of climaxes, keeping something in reserve for the passages of greatest tension or triumph; likewise we must 'space out' any rallentandos and accelerandos. Most important, one needs also to note and to imagine, and then to convey, any emotional or mental changes that are taking place in the composer's mind.

Sometimes one finds that in the course of a work, new light seems to dawn on the composer himself – we think of some of Beethoven's magical passages suddenly transforming and illuminating the scene in works like the Fourth Piano Concerto, written long before his visionary third period, where twice in the first movement it is as if he is drawing aside a curtain to reveal a fleeting vision of something new and beautiful.

Ex 200

Such moments must be seen as part of the whole picture and shown as coming inevitably and logically when they do. Then with tone we must make an imaginative judgment as to the gradient of tonal increase and decrease, not arriving too soon either at our loudest or our quietest moments. In this matter of tonal increase we must be aware of occasional passages in which greater tension can be built up by deliberately holding back tone on, say, a rising passage − only at the end of such a passage allowing tone to make a dramatically quick increase like an electrifying, explosive outburst (a famous example of this build-up of tension by denying an early crescendo comes in the lead-in from the Scherzo of Beethoven's Fifth Symphony to the Finale; the eventual release is a tremendous moment).

One must also be aware that climaxes, meaning in this case the most gripping moments or those showing the greatest intensity of feeling, are sometimes found in quiet passages, as in the great *Arietta* of Beethoven's Sonata, Op. 111, bars 116 to 120. At this point the music has, in the course of a long movement, made its one significant change to a 'foreign' key (E flat major); there is a triple trill followed by a chain of single-note trills rising to a peak. Then, with the hands each playing only slow single notes more than five octaves apart − in two-part writing of the utmost economy − it is as if Beethoven is baring his soul. Surely this was the last crisis, the crucial turning point in his search for spiritual peace. With the last obstacle overcome he can reach out into unknown worlds. In the end this music attains a profound calm which is Beethoven's last word; Op. 111 finishes with the healing of tension, the acceptance of God's will, the peaceful conclusion of the long struggle.

The problem of trying to see a movement or a work as a whole − to feel that it grows from first bar to last, that the sections balance one against another, and that the emotional development is both logical and sustained − considerations of this kind are best undertaken away from the piano, unhampered, in the learning stages, by possible technical difficulties. As with looking at a picture so closely that one only sees the brush-strokes, so a pianist in practising and playing difficult passages can easily become too much concerned with detail; he must be able to view the work in perspective 'thinking the work through' away from his instrument (as indeed an orchestral conductor must of necessity do with his scores).

At this stage a reminder may not come amiss that though slow practice of technical difficulties is often necessary, we are now considering interpretative and imaginative matters and that as too slow a tempo can change the character of a movement completely, it is unwise to play through a whole work or a long section of a work at too slow a tempo for an extended period. This can only result in obscuring the true style or character, making it extremely difficult (or impossible) to 'think' and to feel the work spontaneously at its true tempo later, when the technical difficulties have been overcome. For that reason there is the more need frequently to consider the composition away from the piano when it is in the learning stages. Let this imagining of the work in silent thought mature in the mind to an ideal performance. It is also invaluable to 'conduct' one's pieces through from beginning to end in imaginary performance, aiming at rhythmic continuity and a logical unfolding of the composer's ideas and structure when, in the process of learning, the fingers may still be wanting to take extra time negotiating difficult passages. Obviously the fingers must in due course be trained to be capable of transforming an imaginary ideal performance into reality.

With regard to the development of the imaginative faculty, one is sometimes asked: 'Is it helpful or otherwise to employ picturesque verbal similes for passages in classical and romantic music?' This is a matter where great discretion is required and one treads warily. Here is a prime example of what to avoid: it is taken from comments by a famous American critic of the early part of this century, James Huneker, writing about Chopin's First Ballade in G minor: 'There is the tall lily in the fountain that nods to the sun; it drips its cadenced monotone, and the song is repeated by the lips of a slender-hipped girl with eyes of moonlight'! In this case we shall leave the writer to his 'drips' and to his girl-friend with the slender hips. It may be however that more apt and sensible similes are sometimes justifed in helping us to realize some quality in the music more vividly, but in general: beware of inventing stories for musical works. Musical experiences of the rarest kind can seldom if ever be expressed in words.

Reverting now to thematic analysis: it is well known that Schumann described his *Carnaval* as 'scènes mignonnes sur quatre notes', the four notes being:

Ex 201

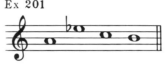

The German names for these notes are A, S, C, H − thus making the word 'Asch', a town in Bohemia which was the home of Ernestine von Fricken, to whom he was at one time engaged before marrying Clara. These letters are also the only 'musical' letters in Schumann's name.

It was certainly a novel idea of Schumann's to use the letters that form the name of a small town and that occur in his own name as a foundation for an imaginative suite of short pieces, but it should not be thought that this was an entirely original concept: Bach, for instance, used the letters of his own name which in the German note-names are:

Ex 202

and we find that the fugue subject of the Chromatic Fantasia and Fugue makes use of these notes in rising chromatic order:

Ex 203

Such examples show that for many generations composers have on occasion taken abstract note-patterns or motifs and with their genius have proceeded to use these patterns to create inspired masterpieces. With such a germinal idea and a fertile imagination it has been possible to build themes which contrast in mood, style and speed; and yet, by deriving from the one root there is a fundamental family relationship which can help to give unity to a work.

In no musical form is this unity within diversity more necessary to achieve than in sonata form. Sonata form is essentially a dramatic form striving to create unity for a movement whilst making use of contrasted material. Through his themes the composer presents the argument or message of his work from different angles. It is not enough that he chooses two or more suitably contrasted 'subjects' more or less at random and, by 'developing' them hopes that they can be successfully integrated into a satisfying movement. There must be some deeper compulsion that causes him to search in his mind for just those particular themes that express what he has to say. Are not these contrasted themes, at times built from germinal motifs of only a few notes, simply 'opposite sides of the same coin', made of the same stuff but showing themselves independently; having a close inner relationship (sharing the same root) though outwardly appearing to be opposed? In other words, are they not related expressions of the various facets of the character of the composer as his personality reacts at that particular time to his experience of life and to the problems of composition that he has set for himself?

The examples which follow are taken from Haydn, Mozart, Beethoven and Chopin.

Taking Joseph Haydn as the first great exponent of sonata form we find in many of his works that he experiments with mono-thematic movements; he senses that for what he has to say there is enough variety and diversity in a single subject which can suggest many possibilities to his inventive mind. A fine example in Haydn's keyboard works is the mono-thematic first movement of his *English* Sonata in C major, Hob. 50, so called because it was one of three sonatas which he wrote whilst visiting England in the years 1794−5.

He uses this theme, which is also heard in the bass as the second subject in the key of G major (the dominant).

Ex 204

Another remarkable − and beautiful − sonata of Haydn's is that in A flat, Hob. 46. Here we find that all three movements are founded on one basic note-pattern which is an ascending interval of the fifth from tonic to dominant followed by each of the descending diatonic notes back to the tonic:

124

Ex 205

The opening subject of the first movement appears as a three-bar phrase:

Ex 206  Allegro moderato

In bar 9 we hear in F minor the stepwise descent from the dominant used now as a new section of the subject:

Ex 207

The use of thirty-second-notes gives added urgency and brilliance, and this is further exploited by Haydn when towards the end of the development section he uses this form of the figure (also in F minor) to build up an exciting and dramatic climax (see bars 65–71).

Ex 208  Allegro moderato

Throughout the movement much effective use is made of a figure of running sixteenth-notes in groups of six; the typical shape of this is to begin with a rise of a third, then to fall over an octave and a fifth, as in the fourth bar and as used again at the end of the climax:

and it is sometimes inverted, as in bar 10:

It will be appreciated that the melodic lines and the figuration alike arise from the six-note motif quoted.

In the poetic second movement (*Adagio*) of this sonata we find this same figure transformed into an exquisite motto theme given to the L.H.

Here Haydn establishes the subdominant key (D flat) with the first four eighth-notes, then proceeds with a decorated version of the stepwise descent from dominant down to tonic. This L.H. theme is repeated and the R.H. adds an expressive counterpoint. In the second half of this movement the theme is treated contrapuntally in the style of Bach; later, there are two pauses for brief cadenzas.

The joyous and high-spirited Finale begins with the following figure, and much brilliant passage-work is derived from it:

One may ask: 'Was Haydn himself aware of this use of a basic motif and variants of it throughout the sonata?' It is impossible to answer, but it would seem almost the more significant if it arose from the subconscious workings of his mind. During the composition of a work certain shapes of notes will be going round and round in the composer's mind and he may not always be consciously aware of the relationships between the various permutations assumed by his themes. May it be said that this use of themes, whether conscious or subconscious, does not by any means guarantee great music; but if the composer's ideas are distinguished it will undoubtedly help in achieving unity for a work, as arising from a single source of inspiration.

With Mozart — we find on examining his Sonata in D major, K. 576, that the first movement is built on two contrasting motifs exposed in the first four bars of the work:

Ex 212

After a bridge-passage leading to A major (the dominant) we expect a second subject of new material but find instead that he uses figure (i) in canon at the octave and at the distance of an eighth-note. Fifteen bars later there is another full-close cadence in A major; this time Mozart commences with the four main rising notes of figure (ii) which form the basis of this section of his second subject. There is no further new material in the movement but it is worthwhile to note Mozart's key-scheme and his phrase-lengths (notably in the development). In the exposition he keeps to tonic and dominant keys, briefly suggesting supertonic and relative minor but not establishing either. Phrase-lengths here are normal except for the extended phrase from bars 46–53 (this contains the climax of the exposition).

In the development section of this movement Mozart explores a wide range of keys in a development of forty bars. There are two canonic episodes founded on figure (a) and each of these leads to an extended phrase. The bar-rhythms are unusual for Mozart, and he approaches the recapitulation with (in succession) three three-bar phrases, one five-bar phrase and a two-bar link. No tonal indications are given after bar 61, but the brilliant writing leading to F sharp harmony in bars 79 and 80 suggests that the brightest tone should be produced in these bars. The irregular bar-rhythms must be understood and grasped if this development section is to be rightly accented and presented.

In the recapitulation: for his second subject Mozart reverses the order, using first the phrase beginning with figure (b) now in the tonic, and in bar 138 (as second section of the second subject) figure (a) reappears in canon in the relative minor. The climax is found in bar 151 (where Mozart uses F, the top note on the keyboard of his time).

A perceptive analysis not only enables one to appreciate the many points of interest, but also greatly influences the interpretation, particularly with regard to tone, bar-rhythms and to the key-scheme of the development section.

When we turn to the works of Beethoven we find evidence of a striving for inner unity even in some of his earlier sonatas. In these his mind seems to be working on lines not unlike those of Haydn, some aspects of whose A flat Sonata have been discussed earlier in this chapter; indeed it seems likely that Beethoven had more in common with Haydn than with Mozart, and learnt a great deal from him. Beethoven's lessons from Haydn were not a success but the influence of Haydn's works is strong.

As early as Op. 13 (the *Pathétique* Sonata) one finds thematic elements common to the three movements of the work, as mentioned on page 100 in examples of phrasing. From this time onwards an increasing number of his works show links between the themes of different movements of a work. It must be emphasized that these are not quotations of whole themes or of phrases from movement to movement; instead it is that note-patterns of three or four notes are used as the building blocks from which to construct themes which may in themselves contrast dramatically. These simple note-patterns or motivic germ-cells are the 'bricks and mortar' with which the musical structure is built, similarly as an architect must know what material is available to him before planning, say, a vast cathedral. With an architect, the choice of material influences the conception of the grand design; with a composer of Beethoven's imaginative vision the conception of the work would normally come first, and there is then the often painful search for the musical material which will give life and expression to it. This material is often forged from simple motifs.

When we come to the middle period of Beethoven's creative life we find in the Op. 57 (*Appassionata*) Sonata that the themes of all three movements (and much secondary material) are all built melodically from the simple three-note figure C – D flat – C. This and its variants are:

Ex 213

(The E natural and E flat of figures (c) and (d) may be regarded as appoggiaturas. All these figures are of course transposed freely.)

Ex 214    Allegro assai

Though in the key of F minor the first phrase of the work opens and closes on the dominant C. This phrase is repeated a semitone up in the key of G flat, starting and ending on D flat, after which there is a return to C. The whole four-bar phrase thus moves up a semitone before returning; and within the phrase the progression from C to D natural in the third bar uses the motif in the form of figure (b), but with the ending of the trill including the note E as in figure (e). The progression of the harmonies in bar 4 should also be noted.

The melody of the main theme of the second group would at first sight appear to have little to do with the ending of the trill including the note E as in figure (e). The progessions of the harmonies in bar 4 should also be noted.

The turbulent figure that follows (bar 51) is founded on the minor version, figure (d).

The basic motif (a) is also used harmonically (and structurally) to provide a bass for the climax of the development section (bars 122 – 132);

and the climax towards the end of the first movement also shows the bass foundation of the arpeggios combining variants (a) and (b): C – D flat – D natural – C. In both climaxes much use is made of the rhythmic figure (shared with the fifth Symphony) of

Different forms of the basic motif are also found forming secondary figures in passages from bar 61 (in treble), bar 91 (bass), bar 105 (commencing in bass and adding the treble) and bars 144 – 7 (bass). At the end of the movement the chords alternating between the hands, with the treble C – D flat – C, provide a powerful climax to the Coda, and the movement closes on C in the treble.

The subject of the second movement embodies the basic motif in various forms opening with figure (b).

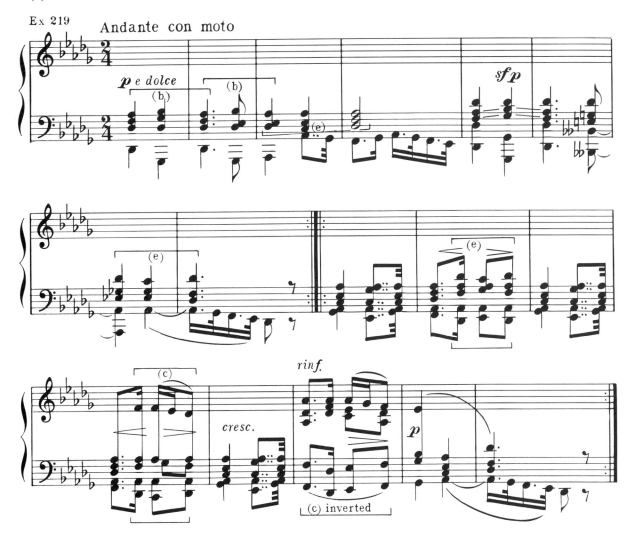

As this movement is a set of variations it is obvious that the same figures will be recurring in varied guises; decorating the third variation we find (bars 58 and 59) a simultaneous triple use of the motif:

130

Ex 220

The themes of the Finale are also derived from the same motif. The introduction boldly declaims repeated chords of the diminished seventh with the treble note D flat, after which descending sixteenth-notes are founded on the motif.

Ex 221 (a)

(b)

The main theme commencing on the note C shows the motif in sixteenth-notes at the pitches used respectively in the first and second movements; and it will be noted that the whole figure is repeated a semitone higher, commencing on D flat, precisely as was the case with the arpeggio first subject of the first movement. Secondary use of the motif occurs throughout the Finale. The bars which are quoted show a new part of the first subject − founded on fig. (a) − played by the L.H. crossing over to the treble clef.

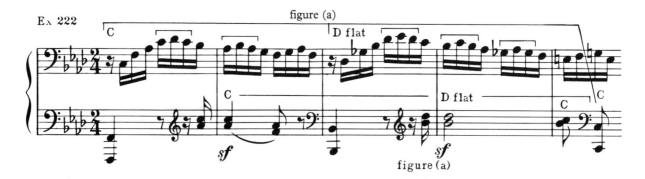

Ex 222

Modulating to B flat minor after the double bar of 118 Beethoven makes contrapuntal use of two forms of his primary motif as follows:

Ex 223

and in bar 142 he starts a new syncopated theme which clearly has the same derivation:

After this the opening theme of the Finale is heard in canon, which is repeated a semitone higher (C to D flat) in bars 158–164; and finally, the coda theme, which gives the effect of new material, is in fact based on variant (d):

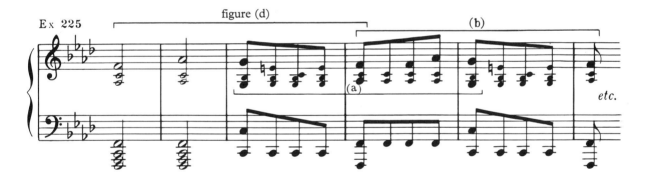

The amazing thing is that this work, which is a supreme example of intellectual organization, gives the effect of being written spontaneously in the white heat of creative inspiration, which it probably was.

One frequently finds in the works of Beethoven that themes which at first hearing appear to be unrelated and are certainly strongly contrasted are found on examination to have a common origin. A detailed analysis yields many surprises and much enlightenment in showing how the themes of a masterpiece can be built from a simple basic motif which may also provide the foundation for the structural design.

Harmonic analysis also should be made of all works studied; this too yields informative and often illuminating results. The succession of chords of the diminished seventh which Beethoven uses to open the Sonata Op. 111 may serve as a concise example. This may surely be regarded as an harmonic motif.

Ex 226

Here he uses in succession the three possible diminished sevenths

Ex 227

and the order of their appearance is never varied throughout the first movement. Particularly noteworthy is the harmonic foundation of the fugato following the double-bar which marks the end of the exposition. The same succession of chords builds up the excitement leading to the recapitulation; and in bars 132 and 133 there is the electrifying effect of two-handed descending broken-chords (in couplets) 'changing step' in the middle from chord (a) to chord (b). Finally, in this movement this progression is heard in bars 146–9 starting the diminuendo which prepares the way for the sublime peace of the *Arietta* which follows.

Ex 228

Ex 228

Is there any inner significance attaching to this particular succession of chords? Certainly one's ears come to expect this sequence and to accept it, in recurring, as still another means of securing unity.

With the greater works of Beethoven one has the rare experience, but the definite impression, that the effect of the whole is in some way greater than the sum of the parts. True, there is often a sense of conflict and a feeling that only by a tremendous effort of concentration and will has order been imposed on chaos; but unity is achieved, and from this emerges in Beethoven's later works a conviction of spiritual triumph. It is a sobering thought that such works are built of the simplest of note-patterns, compelling the reflection that everything in the universe emanates from one primary element.

In the last piano sonatas Beethoven adventures further into a spiritual world of his own, and in the *Arietta* of Op. 111 he attains (as J.W.N. Sullivan writes in his admirable book *Beethoven's Spiritual Development*) 'a state of consciousness that only the great mystics ever reached'. The last three piano sonatas were sketched and written whilst he was otherwise occupied with his *Missa Solemnis*★. They show the influence of that work, and they show his increasing abstraction from the world.

The Sonata in A flat, Op. 110, would seem not only to deal with this world and its sorrows, but also with his visionary aspirations. This sonata opens with tranquil serenity, possibly an aftermath of the uplift arising from the wonderful final variation movement of the preceding sonata, Op. 109. The first movement of Op. 110 gives way to a Scherzo in which the serenity is lost. This Scherzo is in the minor key, challenging, restless, not without humour, violently contrasted – this is a return to an earlier outlook on life that is however no longer satisfying; it fades and gives way to a section of free fantasy in slow tempo which appears to be searching for a solution to problems, but peace and solace are not found;

★ The spelling which is most frequently used, 'Solemnis', is retained here though the Latin Dictionary of Lewis and Short (Oxford University Press) gives SOLLEMNIS as first choice, with acceptable but less correct possibilities – Sollennis, Solennis, Solemnis, Sollempnis.

and in despair Beethoven commences an *Arioso Dolente* (*Klagender Gesang* or Lament). This *Arioso* concludes and leads without a break into a Fugue whose subject rises as if asking a vital question with some confidence. But no answer is as yet forthcoming, and the music sinks back into a second statement of the *Arioso*, this time with broken, short phrases and marked *ermattet, klagend* (weary and as if sobbing) – and it is only at the end of this second *Arioso* when all is darkness and despair that it is as if a distant ray of light is seen: slowly-pulsating major chords commence pianissimo and grow in power, leading to the final Fugue (now inverted) and marked *poi a poi di nuovo vivente* (little by little coming to new life). The effect is that of a veritable resurrection, and from here the music grows to an exalted and glowing triumph.

With the evidence of Beethoven's own markings as quoted (*dolente, ermattet, klagend*) it is impossible to regard this music as other than a human document – the utterance of a man speaking from the depths of his soul; but as a masterpiece of musical craftsmanship it must also satisfy in structural form and sound. How then has Beethoven achieved this miracle?

The first movement opens with a four-bar phrase, the main feature of which is a three-note figure with the intervals of a falling third and a rising fourth. This opening phrase rises to the sixth note (F) before falling back by step down to the third (mediant).

Ex 229 Moderato cantabile, molto espressivo

It will be found that, later in the work, the first fugue is also built on precisely the same figure, but now with simplified, even note-values (except for the cadence).

Ex 230

There is thus a direct relationship between the first movement and the fugue: this gives a strong framework for the structure of the whole sonata, apart from any possible symbolic significance that it may have. Intrigued by this connection we look to see if there is any relationship between the Scherzo (second movement) and the *Arioso Dolente*. There is no sign of the three-note figure on which the first movement and the fugue are built, but it is found that the two middle movements (Scherzo and *Arioso*) both begin with notes falling by step from dominant to tonic, and in both cases the tonic is repeated before falling to the leading note.

Ex 231

SCHERZO

Ex 232    ARIOSO

It may seem that a melodic progression falling by step from the dominant to the leading note is too much of common property to be regarded as a principal theme, but a reference back to the previous Sonata (Op. 109 in E) shows that precisely the same notes (written enharmonically) as the *Arioso* of Op. 110 are found as an important melodic subject in bars 22–5 of the first movement of Op. 109:

Ex 233

This would seem to be more than coincidence and it may be regarded as evidence that the figure in question is, in fact, of some significance.

The fugue subject of Op. 110 has already been shown to be closely related to the opening subject of the work, and the remaining thematic feature of importance in Op. 110 is the inversion of the fugue in G major (key of the leading-note to the tonic A flat). Transposing this inverted subject experimentally to E major it is found that the opening bars of Op. 109 are a free variation of it.

Ex 234
(a)

(b)

Here there would appear to be another motivic link between the two Sonatas Op. 109 and 110 (further links involving the falling third and rising fourth intervals are found in bars 9–12 of the second variation of the third movement of Op. 109 and in the opening of the fifth variation of that same movement). Reverting briefly to the first bars of Op. 109 it will be noted that the first notes of each R.H. group are given quarter-note stems and it is sometimes contended that these notes form the main theme;

Ex 235

but these notes are not related to anything else in the work and it is much more likely that the stems merely indicate the need to hold the notes to complete the harmony, and that the real theme is built from the rising third and falling fourth motif.

Summing up with regard to Op. 110: we have (a) the motif which is common to the opening movement and to the first fugue, and (b) the inversion of the motif as it is used in the second fugue; the motif quoted in examples 231 and 232 is common to the Scherzo and the *Arioso*.

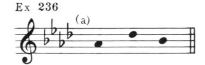 

The first movement is in general serene in its mood, and the ending of the work rises to spiritual triumph. The Scherzo is a physical outlet or outburst and the *Arioso Dolente* is, as its name signifies, a Song of Grief. One wonders if these two contrasting figures symbolize different outlooks or states of consciousness.

That the rising figure seems also to be questioning is shown by Beethoven's later use of it in the String Quartet in F, Op. 135, with the *Muss es sein?* motif. In the case of Op. 110 can it be that the first fugue, confidently asking the question, fails to find an answer, thus leading to the heartbreak of the second *Arioso Dolente?* In the Op. 135 Quartet the question is asked apropos the heading: *Der schwer gefasste Entschluss* (The decision that is hard to make). With the inverted second fugue of Op. 110 the decision to step forward into the unknown is taken (as with the *Es muss sein*) and Beethoven finds that it leads forward to new life (*nuovo vivente*).

Some of the features to note about this music are (from the beginning):

(a) the stirring of life with the introduction of the sixteenth-note accompaniment from bar 5, which quickens to thirty-second-notes in bar 12. The first four bars of the thirty-second-notes (from bar 12) can be regarded as forming the harmonic accompaniment only to the theme of the opening four bars (therefore to be thought of as $A^2$). After this the thirty-second-notes turn into a brige-passage leading gradually away from the tonic to the dominant (E flat). In bar 20 the second subject group begins, but as the whole sonata is built on two motifs a second subject with an independent, contrasting character would be outside the scheme. From bars 20–38 there is what may be termed 'continuous melodic creation', introducing at first melodic figures linked by three high-pitched 'corner-stone' notes – C (bar 20), B flat (bar 27) and C (bar 31). After a crescendo (bars 17–19) on a rising passage of thirty-second-notes, the high C of bar 20 is marked by a sudden 'p', and it comes like a revelation of a promised land after an uphill struggle: there is then a gradual descent to bar 24 before rising to the sforzando B flat of bar 27, thus completing an inverted melodic arch. Next there is a leap downwards after which syncopated couplets of sixteenth-notes rise to the climax of this section on C. The melodic line continues, passing from R.H. to L.H. in bar 32, and a repeated cadential phrase (bars 34–5) closes the exposition.

(b) An interesting feature to be found in the autograph manuscript is that the R.H. in bar 32 was originally written differently. Beethoven has scratched out his first idea and replaced it with the descending scale of the version we know. The last four notes only of this descending scale have not been erased and remain as part of the original idea. We find the thirty-second-notes of the second beat divided thus:

dotted line indicates continuity of melody line

The significance of this is that the immediately preceding L.H. thirds link up with the R.H. in providing a continuous melodic line (albeit punctuated with a rest):

(c) The development consists of repetitions of the opening two bars heard against the background of changing harmonies and keys, as if considering a problem from many different angles or – to be more mundane – like viewing a piece of sculpture from all sides before coming round, full circle, to the front (i.e. back to A flat). The L.H. (like a cello) adds a commentary through the last twelve bars.

(d) Note the three-bar phrase of bars 60–2 in which the R.H. becomes warmly expressive and rhapsodic, before subsiding into the next bar (key D flat).

(e) Bar 70. The key of E major is approached as if it were theoretically F flat major, which explains the E natural (otherwise F flat) falling in bars 77–8 as a minor ninth, to the dominant E flat. The first four bars of the arpeggios from bar 70 are to be regarded as the acompaniment to the theme (unheard) of the opening bars of the movement (similarly as with bars 12–15).

(f) The long half-notes (tied over) of bars 100–3 are an augmentation of the cadential figure at the end of bar 4 of this movement (see Ex 240 (b)):

Ex 238

(g) Bar 114 has in the alto part a slightly ominous allusion to the opening figure, crescendoing to a disturbing forte before fading away to a quiet close:

Ex 239

(h) At the end of the movement there should be a break not longer than is indicated by the written rests before attacking the Scherzo.

(i) The Scherzo presents rhythmic problems of scanning. The first seven bars should be evenly accented, with the 'p' and 'f' markings strictly observed. It is sometimes suggested that these opening bars should be thought of as having the rhythm of a gavotte – which would bring the sudden forte of bar 5 to be regarded as a 'weak' bar. But one must accept the evidence of one's ears and acknowledge the fact that bar 5 is heard as a strong bar. Nevertheless from the double-bar (bar 9) the alternation is undoubtedly reversed to 'weak-strong'. Is it not the case that the sforzando of bar 8, when repeating the phrase, is the link which enables the rhythm to change step?

(j) The rhythmic figure first heard in bars 17–18 is derived from the cadential figure of the opening phrase of the Sonata and from the fugue subject:

Scherzo                        1st movement                        Fugue

Ex 240    (a)                        (b)                        (c)

(k) It is interesting to note that Beethoven writes out bars 37 and 38 as separate bars of rest (not merely the usual sign):

(l) The Trio section is enigmatic. There is a constant overlap and crossing of parts; one part falls from a peak in rapid eighth-notes, the figure of which is based on the falling fourth and rising third of the inverted fugue subject, and which is distantly related to a figure used in the first movement:

Meanwhile the other part (of two-part writing) climbs and leaps upwards to the peak in syncopated quarter-notes. Is this symbolic of repeated attempts to ascend to the heights?

(m) Bars 73 – 5 make a three-bar phrase which throws the normal eight-bar phrases of this section 'out-of-step' (and adds greatly to the vitality).

(n) In the autograph manuscript Beethoven has not written out the *Da capo* repeat of the Scherzo after the Trio section; it is therefore difficult to know whence the ritardando in bars 104 – 107 has arisen. It is effective and expressive, but there is no sign of it in the manuscript.

(o) The chords of bars 144 – 54 of the Coda are to be regarded as syncopated, falling on weak bars. The final four bars of the Scherzo correct the syncopation with a quiet chord of F major (L.H. has a rising broken-chord dying away). The F major harmony will be regarded as the dominant of B flat minor which key opens the third movement. There should be only a brief break in sound before the third movement opens with a solemn rhythm suggesting a funeral march (*Adagio ma non troppo*):

(p) The Bebungs in bar 5 of the third movement are often incorrectly written. Beethoven made a second 'clean' copy of the latter half of this Sonata, from the third movement to the end, because much re-working of the first fugue made it well-nigh impossible to follow. In this second manuscript the text is clearly written as follows:

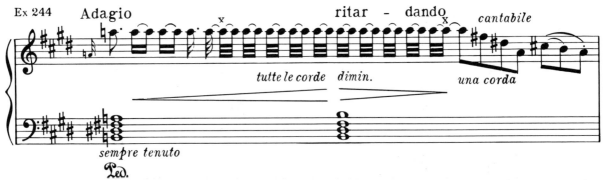

The notes marked by crosses (x) present something of a problem: the first slurs (of two consecutive slurs) would appear to be normal ties, whereas the second of these slurs indicates the Bebung. It is important to observe that there is no slur connecting the dotted sixteenth-note to the first of the thirty-second-notes.

Note that the first Bebung sixteenth-notes are presumably to be regarded as syncopated, following the dotted eighth-note. In the first autograph manuscript, Beethoven comes to the turn of a page when the change of key to four sharps is required, and the chord of B major in the L.H. comes on the new page.* There are five Bebung couplet-groups of thirty-second-notes on the old page, and another five groups on the new page. It would therefore seem that the L.H. chord is intended to be sounded simultaneously with the first couplet of the five coming immediately after the new key-signature. (It should be added that on account of the writing of 'ritardando' and 'diminuendo' the chord of B major has been sprawled underneath the penultimate couplet!)

(q) In bar 6 of the third movement the first four notes of the following example may be derived from the cadence at the beginning of the Sonata;

and the group of three notes leading to G sharp at the beginning of bar 6 may also be related. In giving (vocal-style) separate stems to the notes which follow the example quoted, one wonders if Beethoven had words in mind for this close of the phrase.

(r) Bars 21–24. The progression F flat falling to E flat (repeated several times) contributes to the intensity of feeling in these bars, and the emotional apex is found in the third beat F flat of bar 23.

(s) The fugue must not be played too quickly (a tempo of ♩. = 69–72 is recommended); it should be far removed from the speed and spirit of a gigue.

(t) The broken phrases of the second *Arioso* suggest that this may be taken fractionally slower than the first *Arioso* and with even more pathos.

(u) Bar 132. The turning point of the whole work is the first chord of G major which must be as soft as possible. This is the moment when, after utter despair, a ray of light is seen. From this point there is a reawakening or rebirth, and the work eventually builds to a glowing spiritual triumph.

(v) In the final pages: in the *Meno Allegro* of the second fugue, Beethoven has *poi a poi più moto* in bar 172. It seems too soon to reach full tempo at the bass entry of the octave A flat, in bar 174, and it is recommended that the accelerando is spaced out to reach as far as the half-bar of 178 or even to the half-bar of 184.

*In the manuscript the change of key-signature from six flats to four sharps occurs after the fifth group of thirty-second notes Bebung couplets.

(w) With mounting exaltation the R.H. climbs higher and higher (almost out of the top of the piano), and the final melodic interval is the high C of bar 209, falling to the high A flat of the final bar. This fall of a third is the interval which opened the work: the circle is complete.

It will be remembered that Beethoven wrote these last sonatas when he was also engaged on the composition of the *Missa Solemnis*. That work had an important influence on his outlook and on his spiritual development, causing him to explore a new world of the mind and of the spirit, searching into new regions of consciousness. It was also necessary to expand the old forms and to create new structures that would be a suitable medium for his thoughts. Beethoven's feat of concentration enabling his experiences and spiritual quests to be realized in sound is unique in music, and it is surely one of the greatest triumphs of the human spirit over adversity because Beethoven at this time was completely deaf.

Chopin is a composer of whom it is often thought that he conjured heaven-sent melodies out of thin air as direct inspirations. There may have been instances of this, but more often his larger works prove to be the fruits of inspired imagination and craftsmanship. Perhaps the first of his mature major works was the Ballade in G minor, Op. 23, which was first sketched when he was only twenty-one but held back for five years before publication. Chopin's four Ballades are not in any sense programme music, and they do not 'describe' any events or paint any pictures. It is believed that they were inspired by historic Polish legends recounted by the poet Mickiewicz, and the music expressed personal feelings that were aroused, in the same sense that Beethoven wrote of his *Pastoral* Symphony that it was 'more the expression of feelings than of painting.'

In Chopin's G minor Ballade the entire thematic material is built from four short motivic figures. In listening to this apparently spontaneous music one is not at first aware of the 'bricks' from which the work is made, but their constant use gives a background which makes for unity. The four figures or note-patterns are:

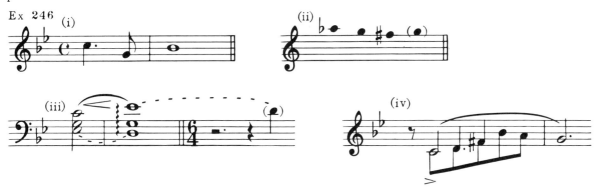

Ex 246

The seven bars introduction in this Ballade may well be intended to be the story-teller's exhortation to gather round to listen (similarly as Rimsky-Korsakov used solo violin phrases in his orchestral suite *Scheherezade*). The three slurred phrases of Chopin's introduction must be regarded as parts of one whole musical sentence: this sentence contains three of the four motifs quoted above, and the fourth is found in the eighth (*moderato*) bar.

Figure (i) is found in bars 34 – 5; it forms the basis of the R.H. eighth-note passages commencing bar 44 where, interestingly, the first three notes are crushed together but are followed in the next bar by the straight version:

Ex 247

it forms a part of the second subject, where in bars 73–4 it is used in sequence, and here (with the falling fourth expanded to the interval of a fifth) it also provides the bass in bars 72–5.

Ex 248

It appears again in the fortissimo restatement of the 'big tune' (bars 112–13), and in the decorative passages from bar 138 it is again the centre point:

Ex 249

The chromatic notes of figure (ii) are used less frequently but they form a part of the second subject; they make a turning point in the decorative passage-work from bar 138; they fill an important role in the Coda where they add excitement to the inner eighth-notes in the passage commencing three bars after the *Presto con fuoco*, and they provide the leading melodic figure in the section starting nine bars after the same *Presto*. Earlier in this work figure (ii) also plays an expressive part in bar 14.

Ex 250

Ex 251

Ex 252

Figure (iii), first heard as the dissonant E flat which has no direct resolution, is all-pervasive. It is a melodic unit, and its use in bar 28 suggests in retrospect that it is also the source for the sighing figures of the opening page:

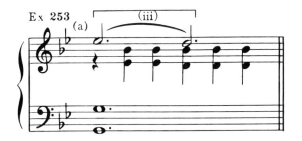 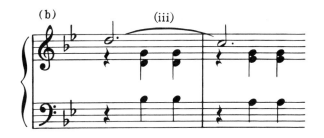

it is also answered in inverted form:

As an important expressive accompanying figure it occurs in every bar from 35–52 and it is heard countless times later. In the two passages built on pedal-points (starting respectively at bars 94 and 194) it is used with mounting yearning and excitement almost as Wagner might have used it in *Tristan*; and finally in the Coda it supplies the frenzied climax of bars 36–41 after the *Presto con fuoco*:

Figure (iv) is clearly the main unit of the first section of this Ballade and as a rhythmic pattern of five notes leading to a main beat it is the basis for the pianissimo passage starting from bar 82 where, in bar 89, the intervals expand and show more obviously the melodic relationship with the opening.

144

This figure is also the main unit of the two pedal-point passages previously mentioned; and lastly in the dramatic and tragic final section there is a feeling of defiant outrage in its use in bars 45 and 49 after *Presto con fuoco* where, it will be noted, it combines with figure (iii) in the final fall from E flat to D.

Of the many other notable features in this Ballade there is the coincidence (?) that harmonically the notes of the first subject figure (iv) build into a chord of the dominant thirteenth resolving into the tonic root position, and bars 68–9 at the start of the second subject give this same harmonic progression.

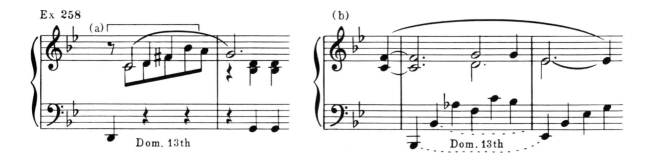

It is also noteworthy that the rhythm of figure (i) as expressed in bar 6 is used to great effect in the ominous quiet chords near the end of the work in bars 250 and 254:

A very beautiful structural feature is the approach to the second subject: this 'lead-in' is an inspiration in itself and it needs imaginative treatment; the horn-call which is first heard in G minor and then echoed in the bass, is then heard a tone lower against a background of an F major arpeggio, and on the repetitions it gradually fades into the distance until the new melody is born. The background of harmony should not be damped through this passage and the pedal will be held until the resolution into the bass B flat (on a very resonant piano it may be advisable to use 'flutter' pedalling to reduce tone in bars 66 and 67).

The final fifteen bars present a dramatic and tragic end to the Ballade. Rhythmically this must not become chaotic and it is recommended that a considerably slower beat of the two-in-a-bar *alla breve* should be adopted from bar 248, with flexibility allowed for the *riten.* and *accel.* bars; the chords of the former of these will be quietly but firmly declaimed like a sentence of doom, followed by wild outbursts of revolt.

The conventional analysis of this Ballade is clear. Significant features are the triumphant statement of the second subject in the far-removed and bright-sounding key of A major; the two episodes, built on pedal-points, that provide such a crescendo of excitement; the splendidly-planned enharmonic change of bars 124–5 which brings the piece convincingly back to E flat, the original key of the second subject (but in this case, is it heresy to wonder if Chopin returned to the second subject in E flat too soon and in so doing weakened the impact of the grandiose return of the second subject in that key in bar 166?); finally, instead of a normal recapitulation of the first subject there is the passage built on the dominant pedal-point D, plus the whole of the extended and brilliant Coda, which remains throughout in G minor, to re-establish convincingly that key as the 'home' tonic.

The use of basic motifs from which to build is common to composers of all periods. In addition to the normal analysis of a work which recognizes its main sections, the interested student should make a detailed melodic and harmonic analysis of all works which he studies. This however must not be regarded as an end in itself, but merely as establishing a sound foundation for an imaginative interpretation, in which intuition will also play its part.

In the case of Chopin we find curious similarities in his Impromptus which suggest the unconscious use of certain patterns. These Impromptus, which may be polished workings of actual improvizations, cover a number of years, from the youthful Fantasie-Impromptu (which Chopin chose not to publish) to Op. 29, Op. 36 and the comparatively late Op. 51.

Op. 29 begins:

whilst Op. 51 has the almost identical figure:

and the Fantasie-Impromptu has the same shape of figure, i.e. starting on the dominant, rising to the tenth and finishing on the dominant (octave above):

Turning to the middle section of Op. 29 the tune of this is:

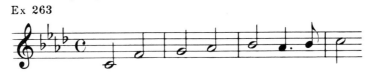

being nearly identical in commencing with a rising fourth then proceeding upward by step to the upper octave in Op. 36:

Impromptu in F sharp

and the Fantasie-Impromptu's middle section is closely allied:

Can it be that over the years Chopin's fingers almost automatically found the first of the above patterns when he improvized (or 'doodled' at random), and that in more pensive contrast he sought an aspiring rising melodic line?

With the quotation of motifs in the works that have been examined the inevitable question recurs again and again: were the composers themselves aware of building contrasting themes from the same basic figures? Expressed differently: themes which are clearly intended to contrast are shown on examination to come from a common source; is this a conscious or unconscious process?

This question was briefly mentioned when discussing a Haydn Sonata. It would appear that sometimes the thematic allusions are conscious; perhaps more frequently subconscious. But is it credible that Beethoven was not aware that his fugue in Op. 110 was built of the same material as his opening movement, or that themes of his string quartets, Op. 131, 132 and the Grosse Fuge, Op. 133 (which was originally written as the final movement of Op. 130) did not derive largely from permutations of the upper four notes of the harmonic minor scale?

CHAPTER VI

# Preparing works for performance

## General

It is a truism to say that preparation for performance begins when one first opens the pages of a work new to one and gets an impression of it – a first impression that may be much modified in the course of time, but that is nevertheless important. After this there are many aspects of studying and learning that come crowding into the mind and that need to be dealt with systematically. Among these are: How to practise? How to memorize? How to present and 'project' – to communicate to an audience? And further questions to oneself: Can nervous apprehension be overcome and controlled? Can possibly noisy breathing be controlled without becoming self-conscious about it to a degree that interferes with the spontaneity of performance? Can any disturbing mannerisms be controlled or eliminated? But before discussing such things a word needs to be said about choice of programme.

## Programme-building

Programme-building is an art in itself. It is of course largely a matter of personal taste and only general indications and advice can be given.

From the personal angle: do not include in a programme too many pieces that are newly-learnt and prepared, whether they happen to be classical or contemporary. The majority of experienced musicians do not reach the stage of being at ease with the presentation of a work until after possibly five or six performances. There is always considerable nervous tension in presenting a work in public for the first time, even if one is fully confident of it in the studio or before a handful of friends; and to be worried about even one work can interfere with concentration and, through that, with the standard of performance of other works in a programme. It is sound advice not to include more than one new major work (or one group of shorter pieces) in a programme: otherwise the nerve-strain is too great.

Know your own capacity. Do not undertake to give public performances of works that contain any passages that one admits are still risky and that may or may not 'come off'. By all means continue to play such works in private, but do not give them public hearings until all passages are absolutely secure.

Make a firm resolve only to perform works with which one is fully in sympathy; and above all, do not undertake to perform works of which the scores have not been seen or studied. This may be hard on a young player who feels he dare not (and cannot afford to) refuse an engagement to play a work he does not know or does not particularly like; there can however be little possibility of being convincing if one is not fully committed. (It should be remembered nevertheless that over the long term tastes may change, and a young player who prefers the 'fireworks' of Liszt may find himself a few years later wishing to specialize in Mozart. The moral would seem to be to keep an open mind, and to try to find the beauties and to appreciate the qualities of a wide range of composers and styles.)

Do not after only one learning put down for performance the greatest and most profound works of the repertoire, even if the technical difficulties have been well mastered. Great art does not yield up its secrets at first acquaintance! – and it is necessary to 'live' with such works as the late Beethoven Sonatas over long periods before playing them in public. A young player should certainly make a first studying of such music as soon as he feels drawn to it and as soon as his technique is adequate; a searching study of such works will help him to gain maturity as an artist, but they will require relearning and rethinking a number of times, possibly over a period of several years, before they can be considered ripe for public presentation.

The planning of a programme requires thought from the structural angle. Whether one is considering playing a miscellaneous programme covering several periods or a programme specializing in the works of one composer, there must be both variety and a feeling of building to a climax in each half of a programme. Programmes are frequently built around a central major work that the performer is particularly eager to play, and the best position for such a work will usually be to close the first half. If this first-choice work is of a dramatic or emotional character it should be preceded by something of a cooler atmosphere, as successive works of similar intensity will obviously cancel each other out to a great degree.

As an opening item it is advisable to begin (when one may still be suffering from 'nerves', and before contact with the audience has been established) with some work that one can present with the confidence borne of previous successful performances. It is a mistake to open a programme, before one has warmed up, with something that requires delicate control and intricate finger-work or ornamentation; preferably it should be of a style that is strong, with notes and chords that the shaking hand can grip firmly!

It should also be remembered that, since some members of one's audience habitually arrive late, do not open with too long a work; it is disturbing to one's concentration to wait between movements of a sonata whilst late-comers seat themselves.

In the case of a miscellaneous programme it is not always necessary to keep to a strictly chronological order, and if one is including a twentieth-century work that is little known, a good placing for such a work is directly after the interval when the attention of the audience is refreshed. A final group (or groups) may then consist of colourful, romantic and brilliant works that are easy on the ears of a tiring audience.

The average duration of a present-day recital programme is something like forty-five minutes for the first half and thirty-five to forty minutes for the second half. With intermission, short absences from the platform between major items and possible encores, the total time before 'lights out' will be little short of two hours. Do not exceed this!

There are many alternatives to the above suggestions, but one has to beware of the juxtaposition of styles that may conflict. It is, for instance, not good to begin with a contemporary work unless it be in a specialized programme. 'Modern' dissonance can blunt the ear of the listener for the inspired simplicity of Mozart that may unwisely follow.

In planning programmes it is also advisable to keep in mind the matter of keys: if playing groups of pieces there should, preferably, be some degree of key-relationship. Major works and complete groups will be separated by audience applause and by a brief absence from the platform, and in these cases there is no harm whatever in playing successive works in unrelated keys. Do not in any circumstances play a succession of pieces in the same key; key-monotony must be avoided. Conservation of physical stamina should be another consideration: do not play strenuous pieces in close succession.

Finally, for the success of a recital, have two or three encore ('bis') pieces ready; if the last item of your programme has been brilliant, a quiet piece of charm makes an appropriate choice.

## How to practise

With a new work the first process will no doubt be to read it through several times to get a general idea of its style and scope (and of its difficulties). After this comes the first serious work on it, taking a limited section to examine carefully the phrasing required and to note the articulation within the phrases. Simultaneously with this it is advisable to pencil in fingerings for all difficult passages. It should not be necessary to mark the obvious fingerings, but with anything at all awkward or intricate the essential finger-groupings should be clearly and neatly written in; write the fingering *above* the R.H. and *below* the L.H. – to put it in the middle is confusing. The marking of essential fingering is a great help in establishing the shape of a passage in one's mind as well as in the fingers, and it can be a saving of time in remembering a passage from day to day in the early stages of learning. It should never be necessary to clutter a copy with untidy fingerings over nearly every note, but do not be ashamed of an intelligently marked copy; and never attempt to erase fingering, unless after further consideration a better fingering is found: fingering marked in during the learning of a work can save a great deal of time when taking up the work again after an interval.

Considering the matter of tempo in the methods of practice: slow practice is undoubtedly essential at the start, giving time to check and recheck visually, in ensuring one hundred per cent accuracy with the reading of notes and time-values. Still more important, this gives ample time for the ear to register the right sounds, which is a vital necessity in memorizing – and a degree of aural and of touch memory should be part of learning from the first day at a new work.

Slow practice however has its dangers if continued too long. Playing slowly over an extended period of time is inclined to destroy a spontaneous appreciation of the character and mood of a work, and can lead later to uncertainty in ever feeling instinctively the right and true tempo. One still hears of teachers who, seemingly as a matter of principle, forbid their pupils to play any part of a new piece 'up to speed' over a period of, possibly, two or three weeks; this must surely deaden any natural response and lead to boredom and loss of interest. In addition, it is often the case that tempo (i.e. speed) determines choice of touch, and practising at too deliberate a tempo over a longish period may be establishing a touch-habit that is not suitable, or may be impossible to maintain, at the real tempo. Staccato-playing offers obvious examples here: what is a suitable touch for slow detached notes will not be appropriate for the same notes played as a rapid staccato passage.

A very limited section, even if only something like an opening eight-bar phrase, should be played as soon as possible at a pace that permits the natural rhythm and life of the music to be realized; this phrase may then be regarded as the 'yard-stick' against which later sections of the work will be measured as the difficulties are gradually overcome. Singing, humming and/or beating time (as a conductor would) will help in establishing this musically suitable pace, and separate-hand playing of a melodic theme can often be useful in crystallizing its character and tempo.

In mastering difficult finger progressions or hand movements the experienced pianist will spend almost all his time on the practice of short sections; not just the practice or repetition of two-bar or four-bar or longer phrases but on the splitting-up of phrases into small units – getting a tonal and rhythmic control of notes within one hand-position, then practising the link from that position to the next. Every difficulty encountered must be isolated, and if a passage (on close examination) requires an unfamiliar physical movement it may be advisable to learn such a movement in an easier form than that presented by the composer (examples sometimes occur involving wide stretches, when it is generally advantageous to invent for oneself notes calling for a smaller stretch, and therefore less tension, in acquiring fluency with the unfamiliar movement). Frequent and continuous repetitions of just a few notes will be necessary if the response to a difficulty is to become as nearly automatic as can be (see Chapter III for comments on conditioned reflexes). Quite clearly the separate hand practice of many passages will be called for, but note also that a difficulty often consists of combining independent hand and finger movements, therefore mastery of each hand individually will only be a partial solution of a problem.

Whilst strongly urging such detailed sectional practice, two possible dangers arise: (a) that the repetitions may become mechanical; to guard against this the ear must always be alert in demanding the right tonal and rhythmic effect from the passage every time it is repeated; (b) that this kind of 'analytical' practice may result in playing that is broken-up into short sections. All such passages of a few notes must be put back into their environment, playing from a bar or two prior to the special difficulty, and continuing past that point. Also, as stated previously, one should frequently 'think' through one's pieces silently as if imagining an ideal performance. It is, incidentally, necessary to be able to start anywhere.

One occasionally hears a student make some small stumble, on which he immediately repeats the passage without stopping to think what caused the defect; and the same stumble occurs again. It should be one of the cardinal rules of intelligent and constructive practice that one frequently pauses (a) to think again clearly what is the effect at which one is aiming, and (b) to reflect and to assess what is the relationship of any particular passage to the whole.

Although the following points do not relate to piano practice in the accepted sense, this seems an opportune moment to mention them:

All pianists should be aware of the danger of developing disturbing mannerisms. Bodily movements such as moving backwards and forwards are not only ungainly but can be harmful to tonal control through leaning on the keys when moving forward and through playing on the surface with no depth of touch when leaning backwards. Bodily movement sideways, sometimes incorporating a rolling motion is also disconcerting to watch and harmful to tone. It may take a long time to eliminate such mannerisms entirely; they should be tactfully but ruthlessly stamped out by the teacher or by friends, and rigorous self-discipline must be applied when practising. Do not however think of such things if any vestiges remain during performance, when to be conscious of them may well spoil any spontaneity.

The same self-discipline should be applied if the player finds himself making throat noises, perhaps of a grunting nature, through tension. These throat noises have nothing in common with deliberately singing the melodic lines whilst practising (which is an excellent thing to do, providing it can be restrained when playing in public!). It is difficult to eradicate the offending vocal accompaniments, and the remedy lies in finding where and when the tension occurs; the assistance of a friend can be sought in trying to pin-point the type of passage which prompts tension and the ensuing noise. When playing strenuously, breathing will be through the mouth, and it may prove helpful, when practising, to decide on specific breathing-places for passages which cause the undesirable throat-tension.

One further word of advice: many players perspire freely during performance. During strenuous playing perspiration may fall from the chin, nose and forehead in which case it is vital not to lean over the keyboard or the keys will become dangerously wet and slippery causing inaccuracy. Remember not to lean forward if perspiring!

## Sight-reading and memorizing

It was implied above that memorizing should start at once as soon as one commences the study of a new work, and it is indeed the case that a new piece should without delay make lasting impressions aurally, mentally and physically (through fingering and touch). Though it is often argued otherwise, thought and reflection on this topic will show that sight-reading and memorizing should be regarded as closely related; certainly they should be developed simultaneously, together with aural training. Whilst sight-reading plays no part in public performance (except on occasion for the accompanist) it plays a very important part in enabling a musician to be what is called a 'quick study' (i.e. having the ability to learn quickly).

The expert sight-reader will always be reading two or three (or more) bars ahead of what he is actually playing. Obviously he has, at first sight, memorized (temporarily) the two or three bars concerned: he has grasped how these bars will sound and where the notes will lie under his fingers, and his eyes are free to read ahead. This, of course, is a continuous process. If given the opportunity to play the work through a few more times, the temporary memorizing which takes place in sight-reading would soon become permanent. It would seem that the view which regards memorizing and sight-reading as in opposition arises from the impatience of fluent sight-readers who are eager to push on to new works. The pianist who can memorize but is weak in sight-reading is generally one who trusts too much to physical touch (tactile) memory and has the habit of looking at his hands constantly; he needs to strengthen his sense of keyboard geography and, if possible, to develop quicker co-ordination between eyes, ears and fingers.

There are many advantages that go with fluent sight-reading, among them the fact that as a musician one can become acquainted with a much wider range of works and can become more widely knowledgeable, and that one can more easily assess the value of new works that one may be contemplating learning. One is also able to get more experience of chamber-music and accompanying.

Though the quick co-ordination mentioned above may be a heaven-sent gift, a great deal can be done to develop sight-reading systematically. Knowing that players of orchestral instruments, who read one stave at a time, are usually fluent 'readers', let the pianist at first train himself to be fluent with a single stave and one line of notes. These notes he must learn to see in groups making patterns (see comments on fingering in Chapter III). He must in addition train himself to read chords as a whole, reading vertically from the bottom upwards (not perhaps worrying overmuch at first if the middle notes of harmonies are not always in the correct position). The most important training in sight-reading is however to be able to look at a short passage and (a) to be able to imagine the sound of it, having sounded the key-note or key-chord; (b) to think what fingers will play the notes, and (c) then to play the passage at once *from memory*, not having previously sounded any note except the key-note. This is the final, vital link between eyes, ears, physical response and memory. It does not imply any special gift, and the development of this co-ordination should be given regular daily practice. Single-note passages of two-bar diatonic melody may be taken first; then take examples with a simple Alberti-bass type L.H. and try to speed up the process and gradually extend it until four-bar phrases can be grasped and quickly memorized (almost at a glance). Playing with others in duets and with other instrumentalists is also a help in the development of sight-reading; resolve to keep going rhythmically, even if some of the notes are omitted in the early stages.

To become an expert sight-reader one must also develop a sense of key: if a piece changes key one should at once think in terms of the new key to which the modulation has been made.

The fear of memory lapses is the spectre that haunts many fine performers. Whilst the gifted young prodigy may memorize easily without knowing how he does it, the adult player will be greatly helped in striving for security if he realizes the processes that are involved. As music is the art of sound it is obvious that aural memory is the basis, and must play the most important part in memorizing; advanced aural training and a sound knowledge of harmony are essential. One cannot regard any work as securely memorized until one can 'think it through' away from an instrument and without the copy. In addition, with the imagined sounds in one's head one must simultaneously be able to produce the physical reaction of the fingers moving to the correct positions.

As stated earlier (see Chapter III), in rapid passages the fingers, well-practiced and trained, will be responding by automatic reflex action. One cannot be thinking of every note played, but the groups of notes will be consciously controlled − which makes it imperative that fingering and touch-habits must be well and truly established. Tactile memory is therefore another vital factor in secure memorizing.

One must also have a clear mental grasp of all structural features in the work that is being played; the work may be an exciting, emotional piece in which one becomes fully involved, nevertheless a directive corner of the brain must be coolly aware of the approach of any critical feature. Typical examples demanding this mental awareness will be found when a passage occurs more than once in a work (as in the exposition and recapitulation of a sonata); there may be small textural differences in the repetitions of a theme and there will almost certainly be new progressions modulating. If one is not fully conscious of and in control of such situations there is the terrifying possibility of 'going round and round', endlessly repeating . . .

Visual memory is strongly developed in some cases, but this would appear to have some dangers for pianists. It can be satisfactory for passages that lie well under the fingers, but for works that contain wide, leaping intervals the eyes will be consciously judging the distance on the keyboard, and there can then be no place for a visual image of the printed page. It will be disturbing to play some passages as if from a mental picture of the printed page, then to switch off this image whilst the eyes concentrate on the keyboard for a series of perilous skips. Visual memory cannot therefore be recommended.

It is urged that as soon as possible *all practice should be from memory*; and in the course of the sectional practice that has already been discussed, frequently allow time for unbroken playing-through of a whole movement or of a long section such as a complete exposition. For security in musical memory a work must become so familiar that the progressions follow each other as naturally as do the notes of a scale.

In performing from memory, concentrate on what is directly under the fingers and on the progressions that are immediately ahead. The 'thinking out' of an interpretation will have been completed long before, and to attempt to think, whilst playing, of a passage that is still twenty or thirty bars ahead will be disastrous. During a performance, let the music flow! (This applies equally to playing concertos with orchestra; during an orchestral tutti, merely know for certain when and on what notes your next entry comes, then sit back and enjoy the music!)

## Hints on concerto-playing

Playing concertos with orchestra is a separate art demanding special consideration. The same skills as in solo-playing are necessary but the approach is different in some respects.

The opportunities for young pianists to rehearse and to play with orchestra are limited; they are therefore strongly urged to seek to play as much chamber-music as possible. If a pianist has taken the trouble to become a reasonably fluent and accurate sight-reader he will find that his friends who are string and wind instrumentalists will be glad to make use of his services.

Playing with various instrumentalists teaches one to listen to other qualities of sound, and to blend the tone of the piano with that which one is hearing from one's fellow-players. It is also salutary with regard to rhythmic matters: the pianist who has acquired a tendency towards being self-indulgent in introducing an unrehearsed pause or comma here and there, or perhaps a whimsical rubato, will get short shrift and much derisory comment from his colleagues. The setting of tempo and any possible divergences from normal rhythm (rits. etc.) need to be discussed and decisions taken at rehearsal. With chamber-music one build up climaxes, or plays in hushed whispers, together: the essence of it is that one plays as a team. There may be the inter-play of a theme being 'taken-over' by the piano after being heard on another instrument; or, in reverse, the piano, having stated a theme, proceeds to add a quiet commentary or decoration when it is restated by another instrument. Such things require anticipation, objective listening and a quick response in adjusting one's tone. Playing chamber-music is a joy in itself, and it is a wonderful discipline.

Applied to the playing of concertos this means that one must know what is happening with the other instruments (the orchestration) as well as knowing one's own part. It is necessary to be fully aware, in studying a concerto, which section of the orchestra is supporting the piano; alternatively one must know if the piano is decorating a melody given to strings, wood-wind or brass. Therefore in commencing to study a concerto one must obtain a miniature score in addition to the usual two-piano reduction. It is vital to know in every bar and every section of a work if one's own part is intended to dominate or to add its contribution to the tone of other instruments and, if the latter, with which instruments the piano tone must blend.

Concertos will in general be of two main types, though there is seldom a sharp line of division. There is the symphonic concerto of which the Brahms Concerto No. 2 in B flat is a remarkable example; in this type of work the solo instrument is treated simply as the most important member of the orchestra. Whilst there are many beautiful and at times brilliant solo passages there is also much 'dove-tailing' with orchestral instruments. The interpretation must if at all possible be discussed and 'gone over' at private rehearsal with the conductor in order to get agreement on major issues before meeting the orchestra; the conductor will be equally responsible as the soloist in this type of concerto for achieving a unity in the conception of the work and in realizing the qualities and the stature of it. This will truly be a concerto for piano with orchestra, demanding full artistic collaboration.

In contrast, there is the virtuoso concerto in which the soloist dominates almost throughout, and the conductor and the orchestra have the role of being sympathetic accompanists. Assuming that the soloist has the musicianship, the technical virtuosity and the 'flair' for such works he will undoubtedly be justified in expecting the conductor to accept his tempi and his treatment of the work. The Liszt No. 1 and the Tchaikovsky No. 1 concertos are examples of this type of concerto; and there are passages in each work in which the piano is expected to 'take on' the might of the whole orchestra and to emerge triumphant. A few such works can be regarded as concertos for 'Piano v. Orchestra' – and this friendly rivalry can certainly provoke much excitement.

The concertos of Mozart and Beethoven contain wonderfully-judged examples of works combining chamber-music and symphonic qualities with virtuosic brilliance. One recalls the delicious dialogues of the piano with wood-wind in some of the Mozart Concertos and also themes shared between orchestra and piano. With Beethoven one marvels, amongst other jewels in his G major Concerto, No. 4, at the inspiration of the second movement with its contrast between gruff phrases from the strings, and tender appealing pianissimos from the piano. One also thinks of the defiant and titanic challenge hurled at the orchestra in the development of the E flat (*Emperor*) Concerto of Beethoven; as remarked earlier, this is surely one of the most powerful and exciting passages in the whole of concerto literature.

Most concertos of the twentieth century are of the 'concertante' type, with brilliant, and often difficult parts, interwoven into the orchestral mass; of such character are in general the concertos of Prokofiev and Bartók. The popular concertos of Rachmaninov are in late-Romantic style with broad diatonic melodies, and much intricate and elaborate chromatic decoration for the piano (a good deal of which cannot unfortunately be heard through the orchestration).

For the newcomer to concerto-playing: there must of course be good ensemble, therefore watch the point of the conductor's baton whenever commencing on the same beat together, and when 'coming in' after any orchestral tutti. Do not however feel that an eye must be kept on the conductor's beat all the time, or inaccuracies may creep in because of lack of concentration on the keyboard; but make a note beforehand of all places in the work where there may be difficulty in keeping together, and watch the conductor's stick or his eyes at these points. It is also good to have a feeling of contact with the conductor when the orchestra enters at the end of a solo phrase, so spare a glance for him as you close the phrase. It must be added that the above points seem to come naturally after a very little experience – though one occasionally meets a conductor who keeps his head buried in the score and will not give the poor soloist a look; and, rarely, a conductor who dreams his way through a concerto with his eyes closed and never a thought of giving a 'lead'.

Some conductors there are who will not at performance take quite the same tempo that was agreed at rehearsal. Let it be emphasized that the soloist must not attempt to play the work at a tempo (either too slow or too fast) to which he is not accustomed. If the tempo difference is slight it is possible to be tactful at the first solo entry in appearing to accept the tempo, whilst gradually and as imperceptibly as possible restoring the movement to the desired pace. If however the difference is considerable there is no alternative but to take charge firmly; make the adjustment clearly, marking the main beats, and leave the erring conductor to follow! – a few uncomfortable moments at the beginning are better than to allow the whole movement to be ruined. This does undoubtedly take some courage from a young player and he must indeed be sure of his ground before acting so drastically. May it be said that the majority of conductors are helpful and expert – and also often both stimulating and inspiring.

There are certain courtesies to be observed in concerto playing: at the end of the performance it is customary to shake hands with the conductor, preferably before acknowledging the applause of the audience. The soloist should also shake hands with the concert-master (leader) of the orchestra; and if there have been any noteworthy solo passages from other principals of departments (such as the first cellist for his solo opening of the *Andante* of the Brahms B flat Concerto) either shake hands, if practicable, or give a bow in his direction. It is not the soloist's responsibility to ask the orchestra to stand: the conductor is in charge.

In opening the performance do not give the conductor the signal to start until satisfied that the stool is comfortably at the right height; and it is wise to depress the pedals unobtrusively before starting, to check that the mechanism is in order. One recalls the pianist who at the London Promenade Concerts a few years ago, discovered during the opening flourish of the Schumann Piano Concerto that the whole pedal block was loose; he vanished under the piano hoping to make a quick repair during the short orchestral statement of the first theme, but was unfortunately still under the piano when his next entry was due. The conductor had not noticed his disappearance under the instrument and, turning to give the soloist a 'lead' for his entry, was thoroughly mystified to find no soloist on the piano stool!

## The problem of playing miniatures

There are in the standard repertoire a number of sets of short pieces which it is usual to play complete (though in some cases there is little valid objection to making a tastefully-chosen selection of one's favourite numbers to make a shortened suite). Before deciding to add such collections to his repertoire the pianist should ask himself: has he the particular mental and imaginative qualities to be able to crystallize a new mood or picture instantly with barely a moment for thought. Remember that in practising such pieces considerable time will be spent on each one – sufficient time to play oneself into the style and character; but in public performance they will follow each other with virtually no pause for reflection or deliberation.

In presenting works such as Chopin's twenty-four Preludes, or a set of pieces by Schumann, it is almost like taking a photographic snapshot of something that is well-nigh perfect; but before there has been time to appreciate its beauty or quality, the shutter has closed and one is focussing on something that is entirely different.

To be able to think or project oneself into a new character swiftly is a special gift – doubtless this can be developed by intelligent application to the problem, but do not embark lightly on the presentation of a number of consecutively played miniatures. Technical perfection is not enough; an instantly adaptable imaginative insight is essential.

## On being nervous

Every performer will be afflicted in some degree by the nervousness that builds up before every performance, and it should be realized at once that this is not a bad thing, provided that the apprehensions and 'butterflies' do not get out of control and lead to panic. Being nervous should key one up to be fully alert and to live more vividly and intensely during performance.

For the majority of musicians the fear of a memory lapse is probably the most frequent cause of nervous anxiety, and the obvious cure for this is simply to know one's work thoroughly from every possible angle. This implies that thought will have been given to every melodic and harmonic progression, that contrasts of ideas (and possibly of moods) in different sections of a work, and that the structure and style have all been fully realized and appreciated. In addition the pianist must have decided on and have become familiar with every detail of fingering, so that physically and technically he is in some measure performing a task that has come to be second nature to him, leaving him free to devote himself to the purely musical and imaginative aspects of performance.

Most performers find the time spent in the artist's room immediately prior to going on the platform particularly trying. At such times deliberately slow and deep breathing can be a help in steadying the nerves. Some concert artists like to arrive at the auditorium long before the concert is due to start, asking to be left alone to immerse themselves in thought about the work (or works) to be played; others, on the contrary, cannot bear to be left alone before going on to the platform. Artists vary enormously in their personal approach and performance, and each must be left to find his own salvation in this matter.

It is generally better that a young player about to give an important *début* recital should not be left alone in the artist's room, but he should shun the attentions of friends or relatives who may 'fuss' or indulge in inconsequential chatter; better to invite a musician of experience who knows when to be quiet.

For the opening of his programme the young artist is strongly advised to play something that he has known for years and is as near to being accident-proof as possible. And it is well that this opening item should be of a strong, firm character, without intricate detail that trembling fingers could stumble over.

Once one has started playing, the remedy for nerves is simple to state, though not always easy to achieve − CONCENTRATION. Complete concentration on the music that is being played at the moment, and a resolve to do it justice aurally, technically and above all imaginatively. At the same time one should be aware that music is an art of communication, and a rapport with the audience must be established. Some performers have admitted that they play to a particular member of an audience as giving a more personal touch than playing to what may seem an anonymous crowd. Whatever one's views and feelings about this, one needs to immerse oneself in the sounds that are being produced; do not try to think of bars and sections that are pages ahead, but allow the music to unfold in its own time naturally; and if the work has indeed been well-prepared the progressions will follow in their right sequence.

Apart from the apprehensions about playing well, there is for some sensitive natures the ordeal of appearing before an audience. If this personal shyness persists one may well wonder if such players are right to seek public performing careers. Certainly they should take steps to reduce, if not to eliminate, this aspect of nervousness. First, try to obtain professional advice and coaching on deportment; the performer must be able to walk on to a platform with poise and without self-consciousness, and he should not be awkward in bowing to accept the applause of an audience. Secondly, the young player should become accustomed to playing before audiences from an early age by seeking opportunities of playing at competitive festivals and competitions and, later, at whatever local concerts may be available to him.

Finally, remember that performing in public is, in one sense, a challenge to one's personality; be determined to meet that challenge confidently.

## Matters of style

When presenting works by different composers it will be realized that a considerable range of contrasting qualities may be called for; consideration of these qualities will involve the difficult matter of 'style' in assessing, for instance, the kind of tone that is right for the works of Mozart in comparison with what one will aim to produce when playing Brahms; or the degree of flexibility that may be apt for Chopin but 'out of style' for Bach. Many such factors need both thought and sensitive feeling; one needs to listen to works other than those for piano, by the composers in whom one is interested. It is also essential to be able to follow the creative development of a composer such as Beethoven who in his major works was constantly exploring new fields.

In the case of the older composers such as Bach, Domenico Scarlatti, Haydn, Mozart, etc. one takes into account the instruments for which they wrote; the texture of their writing and the structural form into which they moulded their works. In addition, one should read widely about historical conditions and about the individual lives (and any influences affecting the lives) of the particular composers; read also the letters of the great composers when they are available, as they may reveal more about character than can biographers of more recent date. All such information can be helpful − remembering that a musician is a student for the whole of his life. Above all, do not play the works of the older composers in a mincing, dessicated style as if they were something from a museum: all Great Art carries its own vitality though its creator may have been dead for hundreds of years. Stravinsky, a great modern who in his earlier life had an antipathy to Beethoven's music, wrote about Beethoven's last quartets, which in his last years he never tired of studying: 'Such music by this most admirable deaf man will for ever be modern. It will never date.'

Many works of the romantic composers call for warmly temperamental treatment that must not however be allowed to spill over into fulsome emotionalism nor into sentimentality. Nevertheless, cold technical efficiency will not leave one admiring the performance of an outstanding romantic work. Members of the older generation were in the habit of praising certain great artists as 'playing with soul', and one can guess at the virtues that were implied in that expression.

## Final remarks

In conclusion, perhaps a few words of advice (or exhortation) to young artists may be permitted:

Do not on the day of performance give a full-scale run-through of a work either alone, or to family or friends. This could exhaust one emotionally if not physically, leaving nothing to give out at the actual performance.

Before the day of performance do not always practise short sections or individual difficulties; save some time to play the works of a programme straight through complete, to renew the feeling of their structure, and also to get an idea of one's mental and physical reactions after some strenuous or tiring work.

Among these final injunctions: give due attention to a few mundane but important matters that can affect performance.

(i) Do not eat a heavy meal shortly before a concert. It may make one lethargic and mentally slow; on the other hand, one does not want to feel an aching void — the pangs of hunger — in the middle of a concert. Most performers prefer to eat lightly (perhaps a boiled egg or a small piece of fish) not less than an hour before performance. Taking a spoonful of glucose (dextrose) is a habit with many. There must be absolutely no alcohol before performance.

(ii) Rest before performance. If a tiring journey on the day of a concert has been necessary, try to find even ten minutes to relax completely — preferably with feet up and supported a little above the level of the head.

(iii) For men: be sure that evening shoes will not squeak in manipulating the pedals. Rubber heels often cause disturbing noise when pedalling on a polished surface.

(iv) For ladies: make a point of practising vigorously in your concert dress. However beautiful your evening gown, make sure that when playing strenuously it is comfortable, that it allows freedom of movement — and that it is safe! It has happened more than once that a dress slipping off one shoulder in public has not only caused embarrassment but has ruined concentration and spoilt the performance.

Music makes an absorbing profession, but cultivate other intellectual and artistic interests as well; one's views on music will benefit from a broader outlook.

As a musician's life is largely spent indoors in private study, seek some outdoor activity, hobby or sport which will help to ensure physical fitness. One is reminded that it was Cortot, the great French pianist, who said that the most important thing for a musician was to have a good digestion; and Kreisler, the great violinist, did not advise a musical career unless one could sleep on trains (nowadays it would be aeroplanes). It is true that good health needs good rest and good food; such things are vital in providing a zest for life — and remember that mental efficiency (and also the nervous and muscular systems) requires a good blood supply if one is to remain in top form.

Lastly, returning to purely musical matters: all gifted young artists must put more into their performances than just what they have been taught, however admirable their teachers may be. If an artist is truly and deeply musical it follows that he regards music as a vehicle for his thoughts and emotions, and if he has been profoundly moved emotionally (and perhaps spiritually also) by a great work, he will feel the need to communicate and to project his personal convictions about it at every performance.

## CHAPTER VII

# Miscellaneous points: do's and don'ts

Quiet endings: don't break the spell by moving too soon. Listen until all sound has died away, then lift hands from the keys (and feet from the pedals) unobtrusively. Make a habit of this in practice also. Hold the atmosphere!

★  ★  ★

If a difficult passage has gone well at performance don't relax concentration – this is just the time when careless slips are likely to occur in relatively easy passages.

★  ★  ★

If a moment of technical untidiness occurs early in a performance, resolve to play the rest of the work better than ever.

★  ★  ★

Don't relax concentration until you have played the last note – yet don't give the impression of being tense all the time!

★  ★  ★

There is often an element of acting in the presentation of dramatic works, but don't introduce obtrusive gestures and facial expressions.

★  ★  ★

When polishing (for further performances) a work that you have played frequently, or relearning a work that is being revived after an interval of time, it is always necessary to rethink and to experience it afresh. It is impossible merely to repeat a success – that way lies staleness.

★  ★  ★

Never forget the importance of 'rests': music must have air and must breathe.

★  ★  ★

Don't develop the irritating habit of beating time with either foot (on the floor or on the pedals). Wiggle your toes inside your shoes, if you must!

★  ★  ★

Echo effects: when a phrase is repeated, do not automatically assume that the second statement will be an echo of the first, thereby playing it more softly. It is just as likely to be soft the first time and more insistent and therefore stronger the second time. Mozart disapproved of echo effects but nevertheless used them on occasions when he considered they were musically appropriate.

★　★　★

Playing of pianissimo passages: successful soft playing is a matter of control, not of weakness of touch. Sometimes practise 'pp' passages with reasonable firmness, and from that tonal level proceed to 'refine' the tone down to a true pianissimo.

★　★　★

Cultivate tonal differences in the subtle range between 'piano' and 'pianissimo'; and be sure that pianissimo is the softest tone that can be produced.

★　★　★

Remember that 'crescendo' means 'becoming louder', implying that at the beginning of a crescendo tone will be soft. Therefore it may be said that 'crescendo' means: 'Play softly! – the forte comes later.'
Reversing the above: 'diminuendo' means 'becoming softer'. Diminuendo therefore implies forte at first, becoming softer as the diminuendo gradually takes effect.

★　★　★

In 'bringing out' a part or making a melody 'sing' above an accompaniment: remember there are always two ways of doing this:
  (i)  Subdue the supporting texture.
  (ii)  Play the part or melody louder.
Generally the first alternative is better, but be sure that the singing tone is not thin.

★　★　★

Octave playing: frequently in melodic passages octave-playing is not the simple doubling of a part: each note (an octave apart) may need its own 'colour' – like instruments of different timbre doubling a melody an octave apart.

★　★　★

Occasionally stop, with fingers and pedal held down, to listen to quality and balance of tone.

★　★　★

Learn to listen to yourself. Only too frequently even a truly musical student with a good ear fails to notice that a chord has not been well balanced, or that one note of a melody has been too weak (or has stood out of the texture too strongly).

★　★　★

Never practise too long at a session without a break. If aural attention and mental concentration start to wane, errors will creep in unnoticed; bad habits may be formed and may be perpetuated. Practising for too long at a time is, therefore, dangerous.

Often practise with eyes closed:
- (a) to give the whole attention to listening without visual distractions;
- (b) to imagine (visualize) where the notes are, in developing a sense of the geography of the keyboard.

In the process of memorizing, realize that memorizing implies knowledge of the chain of harmonic progressions, therefore an harmonic analysis should be made of all pieces and works studied. In performance think only of the progressions that are immediately ahead: the chain of harmonic (and melodic) events must unfold naturally. To allow one's thoughts to stray nervously for a moment to some passage further ahead could be fatal to memory.

★   ★   ★

Ideas on interpretation of a work should come to one from the first opening of the pages. Always be receptive. Interpretation is not something to be added when the notes have been mastered. One recalls the pathetic incident of the little girl at examination playing her pieces with note-perfect fluency, but quite mechanically and all on one tonal level. On being asked by the examiner how it was that the notes were so accurate but that no attention had been paid to markings, she answered: 'Expression is extra, and mummy can't afford that.' The criminal teacher responsible is no doubt still working . . .

★   ★   ★

The treatment of syncopated notes:
- (a) they will normally be played after a slight break in articulation (i.e. a small point of punctuation), thus throwing the syncopated note 'into relief' and giving it a hint of accentuation;
- (b) a syncopated note will always resolve smoothly.

The example given here, and the earlier quoted Mozart Sonata, K.457 (Ex. 99), illustrate clearly both of the above features.

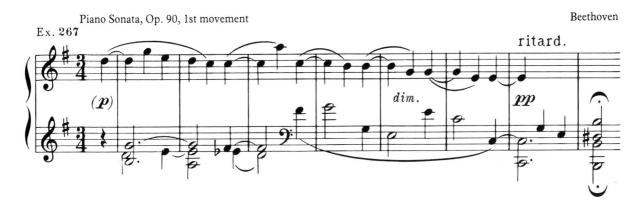

Piano Sonata, Op. 90, 1st movement                                    Beethoven
Ex. 267

When studying Baroque and early classical music take the trouble to learn the conventions of the period concerned.

★ ★ ★

Academic analysis may suggest to the student that music is composed, or to be thought of, in blocks (first subject; bridge-passage; second subject; and the bigger blocks – exposition, development, recapitulation). This can lead to sectional performances: more frequently think of music as progressing through time in continuously flowing movement.

★ ★ ★

A hint on the process of memorizing:
   (i)   at the piano, with the copy;
   (ii)  at the piano, without the copy;
   (iii) with the copy, without the piano;
   (iv) without either the copy or piano – just thinking the piece through.

★ ★ ★

In practising: normally stick at a passage, repeating (maybe at different speeds) with infinite patience, until it is mastered; but with some passages (especially those that are physically tiring, such as loud, brilliant octaves) it is advisable to give them intensive practice in several short spells daily. If outstanding difficulties are encountered, realize that complete mastery of them may take several days, but in learning a work do not allow this to cause delay in pressing on to the end of a work or a movement. Isolated difficult passages can be 'mopped up' later.

★ ★ ★

Always practise to a coming beat: never stop short before a bar-line or a main beat.

★ ★ ★

At performance, how much should be left to the inspiration of the moment, and how much should interpretation be planned in advance? All main aspects (structural shape, tempi, etc.) must be decided beforehand: nevertheless, try to let the result sound spontaneous. Only details such as the degrees of rubato (where applicable), treatment of decorative ornamentation etc. to be left open to slight variation. Never be self-indulgent with main features, but be aware that in the excitement of performance new light may dawn on you with regard to some feature in a work.

★ ★ ★

The statement is often made: 'Let the music speak for itself', implying that the performer should just play the notes and not let his personal view of a work come between composer and audience. It is impossible, and it is not desirable, to be completely impersonal: involvement and full commitment are necessary. Absolute integrity to the composer's text and to his instructions must be assumed, but the personalities of different performers will inevitably reflect the character of a work, and this will be felt by a perceptive audience.

★ ★ ★

Don't resent criticism! If it is constructive criticism and if, in your heart, you admit it has any justification, seek to learn and profit from it. If it is malicious, ignore it.

Remember that a musician needs contradictory qualities in his personality: he must be sensitive or he will not be an artist, but he must also be sufficiently 'thick-skinned' (or philosophic!) to be able to take rebuffs and disappointments without becoming bitter.

★   ★   ★

Never regard any concert, however small, as unimportant. (a) If a work is worth playing at all you owe it to your own conscience to present it faithfully at its best. (b) There may be some young person in the hall present at a concert for the first time, who may be influenced for life by a moving experience.

★   ★   ★

## Acknowledgements

Extracts from the following works are reprinted by kind permission of the publishers concerned.

*Piano Concerto No. 3* – Prokofiev
© Copyright 1923 by Edition Gutheil.
Copyright assigned 1947 to Boosey & Hawkes for all countries.
Reprinted by permission of Boosey & Hawkes Music Publishers Ltd. London.

*Piano Concerto No. 2* – Rachmaninov
© Copyright 1901 by Edition Gutheil.
Copyright assigned 1947 to Boosey & Hawkes for all countries.
Reprinted by permission of Boosey & Hawkes Music Publishers Ltd. London.

*Piano Concerto No. 3* – Rachmaninov
© Copyright 1910 by Edition Gutheil.
Copyright assigned 1947 to Boosey & Hawkes for all countries.
Reprinted by permission of Boosey & Hawkes Music Publishers Ltd. London.

*Canope* (Prelude No. 10, Book 2) – Debussy
*La Terrasse des audiences au Clair de Lune* (Prelude No. 7, Book 2) – Debussy
*Jardins sous la pluie* – Debussy
*L'isle joyeuse* – Debussy
*Ondine* (Prelude No. 8, Book 2) – Debussy
*Reflets dans l'eau* – Debussy
*Ondine* – Ravel
Reprinted by permission of Durand et Cie of Paris/U.M.P.

*Suite, Op. 14, No. 1* – Bartók
Reprinted by permission of Universal Edition (London) Ltd.

*O Polichinello* – Villa-Lobos
Reprinted by permission of Editions Max Eschig, Paris.

## Brief Bibliography

| | |
|---|---|
| BACH, Carl Philipp Emanuel | *Essay on the True Art of Playing Keyboard Instruments* (Eulenburg Books, London) |
| BADURA-SKODA, Eva & Paul | *Interpreting Mozart on the Keyboard* (Barrie and Rockliff) |
| EMERY, Walter | *Bach's Ornaments* (Novello) |
| GERIG, Reginald R. | *Famous Pianists and Their Technique* (Robert B. Luce) |
| ORTMANN, Otto | *The Physiological Mechanics of Piano Technique* (E. P. Dutton & Co.) |
| RETI, Rudolf | *The Thematic Process in Music* (Faber & Faber) |
| ROSEN, Charles | *The Classical Style* (Faber & Faber) |
| SCHULTZ, Arnold | *The Riddle of the Pianist's Finger* (Carl Fischer) |
| SULLIVAN, J. W. N. | *Beethoven: His Spiritual Development* (Jonathan Cape; now Paperback – Allen & Unwin) |